D1386102

My Psychic Stories

EAST SUSSEX COUNTY COUNCIL
WITHDRAWN
2 1 MAR 2023
30

04274368

My Psychic Stories

AMAZING TRUE STORIES OF SPIRIT CONTACT

JAYNE WALLACE

 A GODSFIELD BOOK

To Mum and Dad for everything.
Your continued love and guidance set me on the path that
I'm on today. God bless, I miss you both so much.

An Hachette UK company www.hachette.co.uk

First published in Great Britain in 2012 by Godsfield Press,
a division of Octopus Publishing Group Ltd,
Endeavour House, 189 Shaftesbury Avenue, London WC2H 8JY
www.octopusbooks.co.uk

Distributed in the US by Hachette Book Group USA,
237 Park Avenue, New York, NY 10017 USA
www.octopusbooksusa.com

Distributed in Canada by Canadian Manda Group,
165 Dufferin Street, Toronto, Ontario, Canada M6K 3H6

Text copyright © Jayne Wallace 2012

All rights reserved. No part of this work may be reproduced or utilized in any
form or by any means, electronic or mechanical, including photocopying,
recording or by any information storage and retrieval system, without the
prior written permission of the publisher.

Jayne Wallace asserts her moral right to be identified as the author of this work.

ISBN: 978-1-84181-412-4

A CIP catalogue record of this book is available from the British Library.

Printed and bound by CPI Group (UK) Ltd, Croydon, CR0 4YY
1 3 5 7 9 10 8 6 4 2

The stories in this book are based on real events but some names have been
changed to protect the privacy of those involved.

Author's note

I have been a clairvoyant for most of my life. I have never wanted to be anything else and I think myself lucky to do what others consider simply their job. Every time that I go to work it is a happy time for me and I can't wait for my first client. I get to meet the most interesting people from all walks of life, some with funny stories but most have a sad tale to tell and I look forward to being able to help them by giving them messages of hope, love and joy.

This book is a small collection of some of those stories, some funny that will make you laugh, and some very sad that may make you cry. It will also introduce you to Star, my spirit guide, who has helped and guided me through some enormously difficult times and is my constant companion throughout my life. This is my first book and one that I hope you will enjoy.

My perception of what the tarot cards mean, or what the colours of the crystals do throughout this book, is exactly that, my perception. All clairvoyants have their own style of reading for clients – mine is a style that suits me and has worked well for me over the years. Because I read for such a diverse range of people, you never know, one of these stories may include you. If it does then enjoy my recollection of the story.

So if you're ready for the ride, then let's go, I promise you it's going to be an interesting journey. — *Jayne*

Contents

1

When Jayne met Jade

She was going to be late. I just knew it. So while everyone else rushed around getting ready, I tucked into a full fried breakfast. Now the bacon and eggs were sliding around in my stomach as I looked at the dozens of tea lights flickering around the studio in central London.

I was sitting in a red velvet Gothic chair edged with gold. It was supposed to add atmosphere, and make me look more like a medium, but to be honest, I didn't care about all that. It was comfy, which was all that mattered.

Finally, two hours later than we'd arranged, a familiar face burst through the doors, her arms, and mouth, flapping.

'So sorry, I couldn't get out of my bed,' Jackiey Budden said. 'It wasn't my fault. I went to bed late last night and just couldn't sleep, then I didn't hear the alarm.' Her quick-fire words were ricocheting off the walls.

I smiled. Jackiey was just like I'd imagined – tiny, dinky even, except for that voice of hers – but much paler than she should be, and her eyes had dark circles beneath them. Grief made her look vulnerable, and she had all her barriers up. She didn't trust anyone, I realized. She wasn't prepared to let anyone in to see the sadness swirling beneath the loud exterior. But she needed to drop the act with me now. That was the only way I'd be able to put her in touch with the one person she wanted to hear from – her daughter, Jade Goody.

I'd never met the girl, but I'd seen her on TV and around town. She'd lived near me in Waltham Abbey, Essex, and I'd spotted her shopping or just walking down the street.

I wasn't exactly star-struck – celebrities aren't any different from the rest of us. Madonna could walk in and ask for a reading and I wouldn't be bothered. She's just a person like you and me at the end of the day.

Jackiey was still talking and I turned to Sam, the journalist from the *Sun* newspaper who had set up this meeting. Jackiey really wanted to connect with Jade.

'I don't think I'm going to be able to read her,' I whispered to Sam. 'She won't let me in. I can tell.'

I needed Jackiey to be open so her energy could work with mine. It's the same with anyone I'm doing a reading for – a closed-off mindset, as Jackiey had, makes a person impossible to read. And I knew that would be a disaster today, not for me but for Jackiey.

She wanted to hear from Jade, her only daughter who'd died from cervical cancer on 22 March, 2009, the year before, but she was going to be hard to convince. I wasn't there to pass a test or prove myself. I *know* I can talk to Spirit, but some people need hard evidence, and Jackiey was one of them.

'So, you going to put me in touch with my Jade then?' she asked. There was a cynical tone to her voice, but I chose to ignore it. I should have been offended by her manner, but I knew it was all a front. She was upset really, and just wanted to talk to the daughter who'd been cruelly taken away from her so young. Her cynicism was a defence to stop herself getting hurt.

I pulled out a pack of Tarot cards as Jackiey sat in the velvet chair opposite mine. The lights were dimmed, and the studio looked cosy suddenly, with all the tea lights shimmering in front of us.

'Shuffle the cards,' I said as the camera recording light flicked to red. I tried to forget I was being filmed. I needed to focus on making a connection with Jackiey so I could talk to Jade. And already I knew it wasn't going to be easy. I thought having to handle the Tarot cards would calm Jackiey down, but she was still talking nineteen to the dozen.

'She's scared,' I realized. 'She knows I can really talk to Jade and she doesn't know how she'll handle it.'

Jackiey handed me back the cards and I laid them out in a simple formation that always works best for me, and I kept talking to Jackiey, trying to get her to open up to me. I couldn't feel Jade with us.

Gradually, Jackiey began to relax and five minutes later, I sensed a slight change. She was beginning to trust me, and I wanted to try to connect with Jade's spirit.

'Do you have anything of hers?' I asked, smiling, trying to put her at ease. Jackiey handed me a faded patterned hospital gown.

'It's what Jade wore at the end,' she said, gruffly. 'I haven't washed it.'

I work by using people's personal possessions. I can tune into spirits just by relaxing and asking them to come through, but psychometry – a form of extrasensory perception – gives a deeper connection. Objects hold on to memories, so if you physically touch something that belonged to the person with whom you want to connect, you can tune in to the spirit quicker and stronger than you might do otherwise. That's because the object is surrounded by an energy field, where its history is stored, which I can read.

I held the soft cotton gown in my hands. Immediately, my nostrils flared. I waited, expecting to be assailed by the tang of disinfectant and cabbage, that horrible hospital smell that permeates everything, even an NHS gown that tied up the back. Instead, the studio was filled with a familiar, and lovely, aroma. I sniffed again, trying to put a name to the scent. Then I got it. Jo Malone Pomegranate Noir.

Jackiey was still talking but I was drinking in that scent. It was overwhelming, and then behind Jackiey's right shoulder I sensed a beautiful energy coming forward. It was just a white glow at first, a shimmering image, and I couldn't make out who it was. Then I heard an unmistakable voice.

'Tell her to shut up,' Jade said. 'Otherwise she'll never listen. You've got to be firm with her or she'll go on all day.'

I wanted to giggle, but I was stunned at how I felt. Jade's energy was so pure and kind. As I tuned in to her – still telling me to order her mum to shut up – I saw her clearly. She had a brown bob, and a massive grin. She was so pretty and looked healthy, not ill at all now.

'Jade's sorry for all the things in the past,' I told Jackiey, passing on her daughter's message word for word.

Jackiey shook her head.

'Nah, that's not my Jade,' she said. I spoke again, telling her to listen and that Jade was telling her to be quiet.

'Nah, she'd never say that,' Jackiey said, dismissing me.

All of this was on camera. I wasn't giving a personal reading just as a favour for Sam, the journalist who'd become a friend as well as a contact on the *Sun*. She was filming the reading, hoping to get a story from it – not that I really cared about that. I did readings for anyone who asked, and although Jackiey was trying to appear nonchalant and non-believing, I knew she was like any mum who'd lost a daughter. She missed her and wanted to know she was all right. More than anything, she wanted to be given hope that she would be with Jade again some day.

'Jade's here,' I said, trying to talk across Jackiey. She didn't look convinced. 'Actually, she's right behind you,' I insisted. A look of total disbelief crossed Jackiey's face.

Jade spoke clearly and told me something only she and her mother knew. It was so private, and shocking, that I didn't want it to be picked up by the microphones, so I leant forward.

'Listen to me,' I told Jackiey. 'Jade wants me to tell you this.'

I whispered the message in her ear, exactly as Jade had told it to me, and Jackiey stopped talking for once. She looked shaken. Then she clapped her hands to her face.

'Oh my God. I can smell her.'

She was laughing and talking over me, but she was so happy Jade was here.

'I can feel her,' she cried. 'I can smell her perfume.'

Jade looked so healthy and so young. She wasn't skinny, like she was at the end of her life, but had some meat on her.

Jackiey listened after that and Jade had plenty to say. I liked hearing her, she was special. She had a sunny feel about her, but when she spoke about Jack Tweed, her husband, she became sad. She hadn't believed all the allegations that he'd cheated on her while she was alive, but now that she was in Spirit she felt disappointed. Jade had been in love with Jack, but now she felt that maybe she'd only gone through the wedding to feel like she was a princess. She'd realized how ill she was and knew it was her last chance. I could feel her confusion. On one hand she'd planned the wedding because Jade loved Jack wholeheartedly but she wasn't one hundred per cent behind his motives anymore.

'She did love him wholeheartedly,' I told Jackiey, 'but she's disappointed by all the headlines since she died. She doesn't know what to believe any more.'

The overriding message though, during the reading, was one of forgiveness. Jade wanted Jackiey to know she loved her, and didn't care that she'd often had to be the parent in the relationship. When Jade was young Jackiey had lost the use of her arm in a motorbike crash and Jade had looked after her instead of the other way round. But the pair had an unbreakable bond, and it hadn't been shattered by death. Jade was still there, showing her love, and looking out for her mother and her boys.

I was with Jackiey for two and a half hours and Jade was there for most of it. That showed how much she loved her mum – it would have taken so much energy for her to make herself visible for that length of time, yet she was bubbly and very honest throughout the reading. Jade accepted her passing quite easily. She knew her kids were safe with Jeff, her ex, and she was obsessive about their safety. Jackiey was living in Tenerife then, and the boys would go to stay with her.

'Tell her to get a gate for the pool,' Jade kept saying. 'There's a broken fence or no gate there, and they could wander into the pool when you're not looking, Mum.'

Jackiey promised she would, especially as she was planning her wedding in Tenerife. Jade was happy she'd met a man she liked. She just wanted Jackiey to be happy, which she seemed to be now.

I could feel Jade drawing her energy back. 'Tell her I love her,' she said, and she was gone. I looked at Jackiey. The reading was over, and she was crying, but they were happy tears.

I was buzzing. I always am after a reading, especially when the connection is so strong. This time, it wasn't just because I'd put a mother and daughter back in touch. Jade's spirit was so powerful and so strong, it left me energized.

Jackiey was ecstatic at having spoken to Jade. 'Thank you so much,' she said, hugging me. She was a completely different woman from the one who'd walked into the studio a few hours earlier. Now she was crying and inviting me to her wedding. We swapped numbers and promised to be in touch, something I don't usually do, but I really liked Jackiey. She'd been guarded only because she'd been hurt so much. Now she knew Jade was OK, she was so happy.

'You've got to come to Tenerife. Jade would want you to,' she said. I promised I would, but the wedding never happened.

It had been a long day, but after saying goodbye and driving home, I was still not tired at all. I'd liked Jade and was glad I'd helped her connect with Jackiey. Beforehand, I hadn't been fussed about the 'Big Brother' star, now I was in awe. She wasn't sad or bitter about the cancer, or having to leave her boys and mum behind. She was at peace, and proud of Jeff and her sons. She loved them so much, and Jackiey and I could feel it radiating off her.

So I wasn't shocked when I got a text message from a friend the next day. 'What are you doing on the front page of the *Sun*?' she asked.

I stopped to buy a copy of the paper. 'Jade says she loves Jack but he shows disrespect', the headline screamed.

I smiled. I didn't care that suddenly I was the clairvoyant the entire country was talking about. I was just the person who'd been able to connect two people who loved each other very much and weren't going to let death get in the way of that love. Jade and Jackiey deserved that, and I was just happy to help. That's what I'm here for. I learnt that at a very early age …

2

Wishing on a star

My eyes snapped open. The room was dark and so cold I began to shiver, even though I'd wriggled so far under my duvet I could only just see out. What had woken me?

I looked towards the window, screwing up my eyes, trying to find the usual chink of light breaking through the gap in the yellow and brown curtains. But it must have been the middle of the night because the room I shared with my sister, Julie and baby brother Adam, was engulfed in a blanket of black. Trying not to be scared, I turned over and waited for sleep to come, but it had abandoned me and I lay there, listening.

It was quiet, except for the familiar creaking of the house we'd lived in since I was born. Then I realized someone was in the room. I didn't see anyone at first, but I could feel that someone was there, not far from the end of the bottom bunk that I slept in.

I blinked, and caught a glimpse of a cloud of mist. Was it someone's breath? I wanted to call out in case Mum or Dad had come in, but something stopped me. Peering into the gloom, I searched for a figure. The mist was gone and I saw sparkles exploding in the dark. Gold slivers of light shimmered and danced in the air. It looked just like a sparkler I'd held on

Bonfire Night the year before, giggling as I'd used it to draw pretty orange pictures in the night sky.

'I'm dreaming,' I thought, but I was wide awake, and the light was getting nearer, the centre of it twinkling with blue and silver shards like crystals. I should have been afraid. My heart should have been lurching around in my chest, but as I stared, eyes wide in the dark, I smiled. The light was so beautiful, it made me want to clamber out of bed and dance under it. But I daren't move. I was only five and didn't want to wake up Mum and Dad.

The twinkling came closer, and then I saw her – a young woman just inches away from my bunk. I wasn't scared. She was young – much older than I was, but not more than 16 or 17 – and so pretty I knew she wouldn't hurt me. Her big, brown eyes gazed into mine, and a sheath of shiny dark hair, parted in the middle, hung straight down past her shoulders.

Her face was kind, but she wasn't smiling. She was staring at me, and I stared back, both of us fascinated with the other. A kaleidoscope of light radiated out of her, making her shine. Being in the glow of that light made me happy. It was like being under the sun – her energy warmed me to the bones – and I couldn't help smiling.

Now she was so near I could see what was making the room sparkle. She was wearing a headband and in the middle was a blazing five-pointed pentagram, which was the source of the gold, silver and blue light that shimmered all around her. Her name came to me as soon as I worked out what the device looked like: Star. She said it without speaking, but I already knew it was her name.

'Don't be afraid,' a gentle voice said. I knew it was her, but she hadn't spoken aloud. I could hear her, even though she wasn't talking. It was crazy, but I could hear her thoughts.

'Be strong,' she said. 'You'll need all your strength in the future.' I frowned, puzzled. What did she mean?

She didn't answer but reached out to touch me. I waited for the soft feel of her skin on my arm, but instead a pulse of electricity gave me goosebumps as she took my hand.

I had so many questions tangled on my tongue. Who was she? What did she want? They all melted away, though, as I looked at Star. She made all my fears vanish with her presence, she was so calm and serene, and in her plain brown dress she looked so elegant. Just being near her made me feel warm and happy, as though that sparkling glow from her headband was seeping into me somehow. Was happiness contagious, like chickenpox? If it was, I wanted to catch it.

It wasn't that I was unhappy. I was the second youngest of eight children, and was close to all my siblings, and to Mum and Dad. But I was the quiet one. I was shy and awkward, and lived in my own little world. 'Away with the fairies,' Mum would say. Was that what Star was, I wondered – a fairy?

She was still holding my hand, and I fell asleep like that. When I awoke the next morning, I knew it hadn't been a dream. Star was too real. But I didn't question her visit. I was only little. I believed in Father Christmas and the Tooth Fairy. How was I supposed to know that not every little girl saw someone like Star in the middle of the night? I didn't think it was odd, and mentioned it to Mum the following day after school.

'What did you see?' she asked as I sat helping her make belt loops for the ladies' suits she was sewing. Her head bobbed up and down, nodding, when I described Star.

'She was beautiful,' I said. 'She held my hand, but it didn't feel like holding yours. She wasn't like us, she looked like a sparkler.'

I thought Mum might laugh at me. She stopped sewing, her needle hovering in midair.

'She's your spirit guide,' she said matter-of-factly. 'Everyone has one, but not many people get to meet theirs. You're a lucky girl.' Mum explained that spirit guides keep us connected with the spirit realm and guide our spiritual development. Spirit guides can be people who have lived on earth or, like angels, higher beings who have never been human. Spirit guides bring through those who have passed, so we can communicate with them and pass on messages to those they have left behind.

I was mesmerised by all this and mum spent over an hour with me that day just explaining it all in a way I would understand.

I smiled, pleased. I did *feel* lucky, seeing Star.

'Do you want to come somewhere special with me on Friday night?' Mum asked.

I nodded, glad she hadn't told me off for talking to strangers in my room in the middle of the night.

'I'll take you to the Spiritualist Church,' Mum promised. I nodded, even more confused. What did Star have to do with church? But I didn't ask any more questions, because Mum was busy. I finished helping with the sewing and went off to play.

At the end of the week, wearing my best dress and with

my long, mousy hair gleaming because Mum had brushed it so much, I skipped out of our three-bed terraced house in Loughton, Essex.

'We'll take the car,' Mum said.

She'd been crippled by polio since she was a baby, and sometimes needed two crutches to get about. The Spiritualist Church was too far for her to walk, so I clambered into our blue mini and stared out of the window, feeling excited, as we drove along.

'Here we are,' Mum said, pulling up outside Lopping Hall in town. It was a big, brick Victorian house.

'It's not much like a church,' I thought, climbing up the front step to a huge wooden door, flanked by pillars. Inside, a grand staircase led to the top floor. I ran up it, ahead of Mum, and waited at the top. Then she led me into a large room with plastic chairs arranged in rows.

'You'll have to whisper if you want to ask me anything,' Mum said. 'Just listen.' I nodded, my nose wrinkling at the overpowering musty smell in the room.

'Stay here, love,' Mum continued. 'I'm just going for healing.' I nodded, too busy watching all the people filing into the room and sitting down to wonder what she meant. They were all old. I was the only child present.

Mum limped forward to sit in front of a spiritualist healer, while I plonked myself in the chair behind her, my legs swinging, unable to touch the floor.

'Would you like a biscuit?' a woman asked and I nodded. She handed me a chocolate digestive and I sat happily munching it as the spiritualist healer placed her hands on top of Mum's head. As she did so, I got a kind of warm, fluttering feeling in my tummy. I stared at the healer and could see a glow of white all around her, a few inches off her body. She looked like the boy off the Ready Brek advert, who was surrounded by a radiant glow after eating the cereal, but hers was the brightest white. The light was pouring out of her hands into Mum, who had a dark green aura around her. It was like watching a kaleidoscope of colours merging and playing as the healer focused on Mum. I loved watching the white change to baby blue, then green and back again.

Half an hour passed, and I grew bored. There was nothing to do, except watch Mum, eyes closed, relaxing under the fingertips of the woman with healing hands. Then I heard Star speaking. I glanced around but I couldn't see her.

'Where are you?' I hissed. She answered straightaway.

'You'll be fine,' she said. 'Just watch and learn.'

So I paid attention as if I was in lessons at school, which I'd only just started. She didn't say it, but somehow I knew this was just as important as the words and numbers Miss tried to teach us. I was beginning to understand that Star was my teacher, too, and wanted to help me. I just wasn't sure what she was teaching me yet.

Her healing finished, Mum came to sit down beside me. She looked relaxed.

'Are you OK, love?' she asked, and I nodded.

The room was almost full now and a man went up on to the stage to give something Mum explained was called an address.

It was a lot of boring stuff to me, long words that I couldn't understand. But the woman who came on afterwards looked interesting. She stood on the stage, absolutely still, for a few minutes, concentrating.

'She's going to give messages from the spirit world,' Mum whispered, but she didn't need to tell me. Even though I'd never been here before, and knew nothing about spirits, I could already see a shimmering queue of people behind the lady on stage. They looked just like any other queue of old people I would see when I went with Mum to the post office or the shops. The only difference was that these were translucent, their bodies and faces a swirl of white as if they were sculpted out of mist, or cotton wool. They were dressed in their best clothes, and the women had their hair done, and they were all smiling and patiently waiting their turn.

Glancing at the man at the head of the queue, I heard the name Fred. It popped straight into my head, his voice loud and clear, just like Star's had been. Seconds later, the medium on stage said his name – Fred.

'He needs to tell his wife he loves her,' she said as a picture of a bunch of lilies popped into my mind. 'He's showing me a bouquet of flowers,' the clairvoyant announced. 'It's a message of love.'

Nothing she said was a surprise. I was one step ahead of her. I could see, feel and smell everything that was going to happen. It happened with the next spirit and the one after that. Before the medium could tell the audience, I would get the same message from the old people in the queue. It wasn't scary, it was like playing a game. I didn't understand why only the medium and I saw the old people, though.

'I got those messages from those old people, too,' I told Mum on the way home.

I wondered if I was going to be in trouble, if she'd think I was lying. But she nodded.

'You're a very special girl,' she said. 'Did you enjoy yourself?'

I nodded, and noticed how much better she seemed now she'd had healing. I could see she wasn't in as much pain. I was glad. I didn't like to see her hurting.

I went with Mum to the Spiritualist Church every Friday night after that. At school, I played with my friends but never mentioned my spirit guide, Star, or the old people I saw at Lopping Hall. No one had told me to keep them a secret, but I understood they might think I was fibbing or, worse, weird. So I kept it to myself.

I was happy. I'd help Mum sew, and play with my brothers and sisters in the field opposite our house. They were a noisy bunch, and since we had three cats and two Great Danes, Ben and Sheba, our home was chaotic.

Mum was a seamstress for Jaeger and Dad was a paint sprayer. My parents didn't have much money, but what they lacked in cash, they made up with love. My clothes were my sisters' hand-me-downs but I never went short of laughter. Even though Mum had had her right shoulder removed and her legs were gnarled by the polio, she was quick to smile. Pain hadn't sapped her energy, or her determination.

'You have a gift,' she told me after one night at the Spiritualist

Church, but for me it was natural. I could see these old people as easily as I could see Mum and my own reflection. Even when Mum gently explained that the people I saw at the Spiritualist Church has passed, I wasn't scared. I was lucky. I could see ghosts, and I liked hearing their messages. I loved watching the people who received a message from one of the old people. They would clap their hands together, laugh and sometimes cry, but they were always glad to hear from their relative or friend. So it was a good thing, being able to see and hear them as well as my spirit guide.

Star would visit me most nights and take me off flying to exotic places. I'd take her hand and suddenly I'd be yanked out of my bed, and I'd be zooming across countries and landmarks I'd only ever seen on television. It was always exciting and new. I'd wake up in my bed, but I could smell the desert or the mountain air from our travels.

I didn't tell anyone, not even Mum. She might think I had just had a vivid dream, or possessed an over-active imagination. But these were more than dreams. They were so real, I was able to taste the salty sea spray and feel the wind pulling at my hair. So I loved going to bed, eager to know where Star would take me on my next adventure.

She visited me in class one day. I'd just picked up my glass of milk and joined the circle of my friends sitting in front of our teacher for story time. I was quiet at school, and never got into trouble. Listening to the story, my eyes began to droop. One moment I was hearing about Little Red Riding Hood, the next I was clutching Star's outstretched hand.

'You need to be stronger,' she told me, pulling so hard at my wrist I was hoiked out of my body and soared upwards. Holding on to her hand, I was flying above my classmates, so high I could touch the ceiling. I glanced down at my teacher, still reading the story, and the girls and boys, listening attentively. I could see myself, dozing in the corner, my eyes closed. It felt weird to be watching myself, knowing I was in two places at once.

I was having an out-of-body experience, and had been astral travelling for weeks, but right now it just felt like fun. I didn't question my own or Star's abilities. It felt normal to be with her, playing ring-o-ring-o-roses above my class, giggling and spinning until my loose hair flew behind me and my eyes watered.

'Jayne!' The teacher shouted my name so loud I was jolted back into my body.

'Home time,' she snapped as I blinked, trying to focus. I felt fuzzy and tired, and was terrified she'd realize what had happened and tell me off.

'Sorry, Miss,' I mumbled, vowing never to fall asleep in class again.

'No more visits at school,' I scolded Star when she came to see me the next night. I didn't want my teacher to tell my mum I wasn't paying attention.

My parents took education seriously and wouldn't have been happy if they thought I wasn't doing my best. I didn't want Mum to think the Spiritualist Church or Star were getting in the way of school, so I worked extra hard, practising my writing and my times tables. It was only at night that I could relax, knowing that Star would visit, bringing different people to meet me from the spirit world. They were swirls of colour at first, who would gradually shift into focus and become people, young and old.

'You're going to see the world,' Star would tell me. 'You'll be someone special.'

I'd shrug, a bit embarrassed. I didn't feel special. I was just average. What could I do? But over the months since we'd met, Star was helping me. She wanted me to listen to my inner voice, the one connected to Spirit. I needed to fine-tune it so I could hear everyone who needed to talk to me. I heard her voice – it was soft, like a piano tinkle, but her words were serious, driving me on to take in everything she was saying.

I accepted the spirits she brought to see me, listened to my intuition when they spoke. They didn't talk out loud. I heard them in my mind, and in my feelings. Star was teaching me to listen to my inner voice, so I could pick up every meaning in their messages, and talk to them when I wanted to, not just when they chose. It's like when you're thinking about a friend and wishing that person would call and suddenly the phone rings and it's your buddy. That's how the spirits talked to me. I'd sense what they wanted to say, and as I practised with Star, it became easier and easier, until I didn't have to concentrate at all. I could just understand without even trying.

It seeped into every part of my life then. I couldn't shut it off. I hadn't learnt how to, even though Star kept my spiritual lessons going all the time. There was just so much to take in, but my intuition was becoming stronger. I was only skinny, and I thought I'd topple over if I tried to resist the very real, magnetic pull I felt to help someone who needed it. I'd know just by looking, and I couldn't ignore it. So I'd go and sit with the girl who was being bullied, or play bulldog with the boy who was being hit by his drunken dad.

I never said anything about the messages I received, but just tried to help in my own little way. I wanted to make the person feel better. Sometimes it was hard not to say the wrong thing accidentally, though, especially if I didn't know that what I was seeing or feeling was a spirit message.

'Your nan really loves you,' I blurted out to a girl in class one day. 'She wants to bake more cakes for you.'

My classmate burst into tears and told me her nan had passed away the night before. That made me wary of saying what I felt, but mostly it was impossible to ignore.

'Fancy going for a walk?' Mum asked one Sunday. She was going to take the dogs over to High Beach, in Epping Forest, before lunch, and so I tagged along with her. I was 10 now, and as soon as we got out of the car, and I spotted a church nearby, I sensed Star was there. I didn't even need to see her any more, our bond was so strong.

'You'll need to be very strong soon,' she told me as I headed into the graveyard while Mum watched the dogs. 'Something is coming that will really test you.'

I looked around, scared, but she didn't mean right now.

'It's in the future,' she said. 'But you will need all the strength you've got.'

I stopped. A girl was watching me from the corner of the

graveyard. I'd just seen her come from around the back of the church, her blonde curls bobbing. I knew immediately she was a spirit. Her face was beautiful but too pale, and her blue eyes were like chips of ice. She wore a white dress, white tights and white shoes.

'Do you want to play?' she asked, darting between the headstones. I nodded, but grew tired after a bit, so we sat on the grass looking at each other. She told me her name was Rosie, and she looked a similar age to me.

'I'm so happy,' she said. 'No one usually sees me, so they never play with me.' I smiled back, glad I'd come.

'See you next Sunday?' I said, when Mum called me back to the car.

Rosie was always waiting when I turned up. Every week I took dollies and toys to play with her. Mum never questioned me. She'd sit on a bench, having a flask of tea, watching the dogs scamper off into the woods, while I'd catch up with my new-found friend.

'I'm here with my mum,' Rosie said one day, and I nodded, feeling her sadness. I expected her to point out her headstone but she never did. I don't think she was aware that she'd passed over. Rosie was nine and liked having another little girl to play with.

Maybe it was because of my friendship with Rosie, or my lessons with Star, but my connection with Spirit was getting stronger and stronger. I could see an aura surrounding most people now, and loved watching the sparkling rainbow of colours around children and babies. I think maybe I always had seen them, but they'd been faint. I never questioned that everyone had a colourful aura, and thought everyone could see them. Everyone could see that people's eyes were different colours, so why wouldn't they see the beautiful hues surrounding people?

I didn't understand how special my gift was. How could I? All the mediums at the Spiritualist Church could see auras and spirits, so why would I stand out? It was as normal for me to watch clairvoyants pass on messages from the dead as it was for most people to watch 'Coronation Street'. I just accepted it as part of life, something that would always be there as I grew up to be an athlete or a nurse.

And then one day, not long after I met Rosie, Mum and I went to the Spiritualist Church and watched a man give a psychometry demonstration. He used people's possessions, such as a watch or a ring, to pick up messages from Spirit and details about the owner. Now I know that touching such an item gives the medium something tangible to work with, and we all know that objects pick up the energy of the people who wear them. That's why some items of jewellery or clothes are considered lucky. On that day, I watched this man reel off message after message, without missing a beat. He knew incredible details and gave names, which were always spot on. He had my full attention. I was impressed. He was far more detailed than anyone I'd ever seen before. 'I want to be able to do that,' I thought. People were crying and clapping at the end of his session because it had been so amazing.

'Can we go and talk to him?' I begged Mum and rushed over. He asked if I could talk to Spirit. When I nodded, he handed me a watch. I jolted, the energy coming off it was so strong. It was the difference between watching a TV in black and white and then in colour with 3-D. I could see, smell and feel the owner, a beautiful young woman with red hair. I didn't have to think hard. Instantly, I knew her name was Susan and that she had a very strange message that she was saying over and over: 'I miss the plant pot that was by the window.' It made no sense to me, but the man looked shocked.

'She was my daughter,' he said, 'and I've just moved a plant pot that she used to sit by to look out of the window.'

I handed back the watch, amazed that I could do this. The man turned to my mum, asking her to keep encouraging me.

'You'll be doing this in ten years' time,' he said to me. 'I think you're a natural.'

I smiled, pleased to have made Mum proud, but I wasn't so sure this was going to be a career. What was I supposed to say when people asked what I did for a living – 'Oh, I talk to ghosts'? Everyone would think I was bonkers. So I practised psychometry and listening to my inner voice, but when I wasn't playing with Rosie or at the church with Mum, I was like any normal girl. I watched 'Blue Peter' on TV, and began experimenting with my older sister Julie's make-up when she wasn't around.

'Be strong,' Star would say whenever she visited me. I sensed an urgency in her voice as the months passed.

'Why?' I asked her every time, but she never answered. Unfortunately, I didn't have long to wait until I found out.

3

Lost and found

I couldn't breathe. My lungs were burning as I battled to gulp in some air. Pain knifed through my right hip and I wanted to cry out, but couldn't. I was in so much agony, I'd stopped breathing in my sleep. Now, silently sobbing, I waited for my lungs to stop screaming.

'Breathe in,' I told myself as my shoulders heaved, 'blow out.' I was panting now, but it felt as though my right hip was on fire. I tried to get out of bed, but couldn't stand. My hip had locked, and I couldn't put my right foot on the floor.

'Help me,' I finally managed to croak, and my sister Julie heard.

'What's the matter?' she asked, shocked to see me crying.

'I can't walk,' I sobbed. 'It hurts.' She ran to fetch my parents.

'What is it, love?' Mum said. I told her as Dad carried me downstairs to the sofa. Mum called the doctor.

'He says to take her to hospital,' she said, grabbing a coat to put round me.

I couldn't even hobble to the car. Dad had to pick me like a little girl, even though I was 13. Lying on the back seat, I screamed when we went over any bumps on the way to the hospital. I'd never experienced pain like this. It was as if someone was sawing through my right hip.

'Help me,' I yelled, my entire body shaking. 'Give me something for the pain.'

I'd never been in a hospital before, and blinked under the glaring overhead lights. I was fighting to keep control as pain sliced through me again and again. Eventually, doctors gave me an injection to numb it, and I lay back, exhausted. Then they sent me for an X-ray, a scan and blood tests.

'We can't find anything wrong,' the doctor told Mum and Dad. 'Maybe it's groin strain.'

I would have laughed if I hadn't been in so much agony. A keen runner, I competed for my school, Luckton Girls in Loughton, and I also did gymnastics and swimming. I'd pulled enough muscles and had enough strains to know that this was something serious.

'It really hurts, Mum,' I croaked, and she squeezed my hand. She knew I didn't complain usually.

'There has to be something you can do,' she pleaded.

So after a conflab, the doctors decided to give me painkillers, and put my right leg in traction, in case the hip joint had popped out of its socket.

'It's the only way to realign the hip,' the consultant said.

I had to lie flat in a hospital bed, staring at the ceiling, while weights were attached to a pulley system on my leg. I thought it would take away the pain, but it was torture. Now, as well as the stabbing pains, I had a gnawing ache where the hip was being yanked out. I couldn't move, or think straight.

'Take these,' the nurse would say, handing me white painkillers.

I needed more and more to cope with the pain and, eventually, I was taking twelve a day, which was making my stomach sore.

'You've got to eat,' she'd urge, but I'd lost my appetite. I could never stomach anything if I didn't feel well. One day passed, then another and another.

'Come on, love,' Mum urged, bringing in fruit and Lucozade. But just the thought of eating made me feel sick. As I stared at the bowl of fruit on the tray at the end of my bed, my stomach began to gurgle. 'Oh no,' I thought, my mouth flooding with sour saliva. Too late. I opened my mouth to speak, and vomited all down myself, and once I started I couldn't stop.

'She's allergic to the painkillers,' the doctor told Mum, giving me anti-sickness drugs and switching my tablets.

The next day I stopped puking, but I felt worse than ever, and still couldn't eat. I was naturally skinny, and now looked dreadful. Within a week my brown shiny hair hung lank around my pale face. My eyes were sunken with dark, black circles underneath, and there wasn't a spare ounce of fat on me.

'We've come to give you your dinner, young lady,' a nurse said later that day after Mum and Dad had gone. She was carrying a large tray of food, and another nurse and a male auxiliary were trailing behind her. I opened my mouth to protest, and suddenly felt two hands on my shoulders, pinning me down. Another pair of hands caught my flailing arms and the nurse, her face pinched in determination, shovelled a spoonful of mashed potato into my mouth. I gagged, and began to choke, but they didn't let go. Panicking, I forced myself to swallow, tears escaping from the corner of my eyes. The smell, and lumpy texture, made me retch, but still the spoons kept on coming. The nurse was force-feeding me, and it was all I could do to stop myself from throwing up.

'It's for your own good,' she said, thinking she was doing her job properly and getting me to eat. But she gave me a fear of mashed potato and hospitals that still lingers today. As soon as I see it, I get flashbacks to those three adults holding me down, and I panic, knowing I'm going to choke. I'd rather stick pins in my eyes than eat a spoonful of mashed spuds.

I was determined to get out of hospital after that. I should have said something to Mum when she came in at visiting time, but I didn't want to worry her even more. So I tried to be brave, and forced myself to eat as much food as I could to keep that nasty nurse and her two side-kicks away.

However, Mum had been doing some research into what could possibly be wrong with me, and had read about juvenile rheumatoid arthritis in one of her medical books.

'Test her for that,' she begged the doctors. It came back negative. 'Do it again,' Mum insisted day after day, and the doctors relented, probably just to shut her up. It was lucky she'd gone on, though, because the next time the result was positive. I had juvenile rheumatoid arthritis (JRA), a chronic autoimmune disease that attacks and eventually destroys the joints. Once under attack, they swell, which causes the pain. It would never go away, and would gradually work its way round my body to all my joints, deforming them.

'You'll never be able to run again,' the specialist said. I flinched. He might as well have told me I had six months to live.

I loved running and sports. It was what I was good at. I always came first or second, and loved the way I could switch off my mind, and Star, as I ran or swam or leapt over the horse. I was only 13, and had dreamt of being an athlete. Now all that was being taken away from me. What was I going to do?

Is this what Star had warned me about and prepared me for all these years? To tell a teenager she can no longer do the thing she loves most, and that she might end up in a wheelchair, is so cruel. Why couldn't she have come straight out with the truth? Maybe I could have prevented it or gone to see a doctor earlier. If she was so amazing, and cared about me at all, why couldn't she have stopped it or found a cure? What sort of spirit guide was she, allowing this to happen? And where had she been when I'd been in so much pain? I hadn't felt her around me since this started. Was she too ashamed to face me?

'Well, I hate you, Star,' I raged. 'I never want to hear or see you again.' She was spiteful, and in my pain and fury, I vowed never to allow her in again. I'd spent years opening up to her so that I could see and listen to her, and Spirit. I'd been developing my psychic communication, and learning to trust my instincts and intuition. Now, as if I was flicking a switch, I closed it off. 'Never again,' I kept telling myself, bitterly. I didn't need her. She hadn't helped me when I really needed her. I'd manage fine on my own.

So that was it. I shut her out, and spent all my energy keeping her out. There were times over the next few days and weeks I could feel Star desperately trying to come through to communicate. I refused to listen. She wasn't my spirit guide any more. To me, she didn't exist.

Instead, I focused on having hydrotherapy in the hospital swimming pool and intense physio. The traction had pulled my right hip out of its socket, leaving me in even more pain than when I was admitted. It was so inflamed and stiff, I couldn't put any weight on it, and needed to learn to walk again. Every step was agony, but I persevered, because that was the only way I was going to be allowed home. Finally, I could walk unaided and was discharged from hospital.

It had been two and a half weeks, but it seemed like forever. So much had happened. I'd gone into hospital a little girl, and had come out an angry young woman. I felt betrayed by Star and was embarrassed about my condition. JRA was debilitating, as well as painful, and it had hit me at the worst time. All girls of my age cared about was make-up, and fitting in. Now I was officially a freak.

I didn't want anyone to know about it. I wasn't disabled. I wanted to be treated like everyone else. But I sank into a deep depression. Back home, I lay in bed, sulking or crying, feeling sorry for myself. And the pain was so intense I couldn't cope. The hospital had given me morphine to take but it didn't kill it completely. I'd beg my little brother, Adam, who was only nine, to massage my joints for hours on end, and I refused to go to school.

'The other girls will laugh at me,' I told Mum.

She persuaded me to go back but one of the other girls on the running team, whom I'd always beaten, poked fun at me.

'Cripple,' she spat. 'You're just like your mum now.'

Fury exploded through me. I fled home in tears.

'I'm never going back,' I yelled, banging the front door shut, and slamming up to my bedroom.

Mum rang the education authority, who paid for me to go to a private tutor, ten minutes' drive away. She taught me the basics of English and Maths, but mostly we cooked. I didn't mind. It was relaxing and meant she always had tea ready for when her kids got in. My unofficial cookery school didn't last long, though. I came home one day and Mum handed me a letter. I was being sent to a school for kids with emotional problems, or who just refused to go to the local comprehensive. To be honest, I was dreading it, but it was better than I'd expected. I was dopey from all the drugs I was on, but I fitted in fine and soon made friends.

Then, when I was 15, Mum dropped a bombshell. She was leaving Dad. 'We still love each other but we've grown apart,' she said as I cried. Dad was devastated, but Mum sold the family home and moved out, taking Adam and me with her. The rest of my brothers and sisters were older and had already scattered. So from a house full of noise and chaos, we moved to a place of quiet and order. I missed everyone being together, but I couldn't mope around for too long. My pain was so bad, I had to keep busy to take my mind off it.

After a while, I accepted Mum and Dad's split. Mum was happier having her independence and they were still friends, seeing each other all the time, and having family get-togethers. It was odd at first, but gradually we all got used to it.

For a while, I felt normal, like everyone else, but it took all my effort to keep that psychic button firmly switched to off. I wasn't admitting Star after the way she'd let me down. One night I was out with my friend Anita and bumped into her boyfriend Lee and his friend, Simon.

'Why don't you come with us to Southend for the day tomorrow?' Anita asked, and I agreed.

Simon was a little older than I was, and I was shy and awkward because of my illness. But Simon didn't notice my swollen, misshapen fingers, wrists and elbow joints, or if he did, he didn't say anything. We went on the roller-coasters, giggling together, and later sat in the back of Lee's car holding hands.

Simon was sweet and good to me. He was handsome, too, six foot tall with curly brown hair, and a kind face. We dated for a year before I moved in with him. 'I love you,' he told me one day. 'Marry me?'

Of course, with hindsight, I can see I should have said no. We were too young. He was my first boyfriend. It was too soon. Mum, Dad, my friends and brothers and sisters were all telling me not to go ahead, but I was fed-up with being bossed around by doctors, nurses and my family. This was my way of proving I was grown-up and could do as I wanted.

'We're getting married and nothing you say can stop that,' I announced.

So, at 17, I married the first boy I'd kissed. I beamed as I walked into Epping Register Office in my peach and cream silk dress in front of my parents, family and friends. They didn't agree with me marrying Simon, but they came when I refused to give in.

'You look beautiful,' Mum whispered.

I thought I was a woman, getting married, but I was still a little girl. I always giggle when I'm nervous, and I fluffed my vows, I was laughing so much. Simon didn't care, and stared into my eyes as he slipped a gold band on to my wedding finger. Luckily, the juvenile rheumatoid arthritis had mostly attacked my right side, deforming the joints on the fingers of my right hand, right hip and both elbows.

The reception was at my sister Lorraine's house. Mum had paid for a big cake and champagne. We couldn't afford a honeymoon. I went back to work the next day, running a bed and breakfast establishment for a businessman in Woodford, Essex.

It was boring and hard work, but it put a roof over our heads. Being married wasn't anything special. I thought it would be more exciting than just living together, but, of course, Simon was the same man he'd been before – quiet. He spent all his spare time watching TV, and I missed Mum. She didn't come round as often now I was a married woman. She announced she was going to Tenerife for three months because her polio was so bad. She knew the sun would stop her legs aching. I wanted her to feel better but, selfishly, I didn't want her to go. I'd already tired of being with Simon all the time. I'd chatter on and he'd just nod. We were 17 going on 70.

So I watched Mum go with Dad – they were still so close they even went on holiday together, even though they were divorcing – and being without them made me realize I didn't want to be Simon's wife any more. 'It was a mistake,' I told him. 'I should have listened to my mum.' He didn't think I was serious when I said I was leaving, but I packed my stuff and walked out. We'd lasted less than a year.

I was on morphine because the pain in my joints was so bad, so I headed off to find Mum and Dad in Tenerife. Mum's idea of getting the sun on your body to ease the aches and pains was a good one. I paid for it by selling my Volvo car, my pride and joy. 'That'll keep me going out there for a while,' I figured. So I filed for divorce on the grounds of irretrievable breakdown and bought a plane ticket.

I left all the hassle of Simon behind and within days the pain in my joints had almost gone. I felt young again, not like a crippled old lady. Even when Mum and Dad went home, I stayed on and invested my car money in a bar in Las Americas with an old family friend, Colin Booker. My self-confidence along with my health bounced back under the blue skies. For once, I had no worries. I shared an apartment with my friends Kerry and Angie, worked behind the bar until late, then partied. I was catching up on years of fun I'd missed out on because of the juvenile rheumatoid arthritis.

I loved Tenerife. It was hot, and everyone was in a good mood because they were either on holiday, or felt as though they were, even if, like me, they were living and working there. We all knew how lucky we were to have escaped the drizzle back home in Britain, and so everyone made the most of every day. My body unfurled under the sun, which warmed my bones and made my joints hurt less and less each month, until I sometimes forgot I had JRA.

There was a good energy there, too. Life seemed easy. You woke up, ate simple but tasty food, lay on the beach, splashed in the warm sea and made friends. Within a year, I'd come out of my shell, and knew everyone on the island. 'Nothing can spoil this,' I thought, sitting on the beach one day, the sun warming my face. But in the early hours of the next day the phone rang.

'Hello,' I said, still half-asleep. It was 4am.

'Jayne. Get home now,' Adam said. 'Mum's dead.'

The room span in the dark. I could feel myself swaying in bed. My hand was gripping the receiver so tightly, my knuckles locked.

'Did you hear me?' Adam asked, panic in his voice.

'Yes,' I mumbled. 'I'm on my way.' I hung up, then burst into tears. 'I need to get home now,' I thought, trying to work out what to do. But I couldn't think straight. How could Mum be dead? She was only 52. I pulled on some clothes, scrabbling around for my bag, and chucking random items into it.

'I need to get to London now,' I told a woman at the check-in desk at the airport. 'My mum's dead.' But she didn't have any direct flights to anywhere in the UK for four days.

I was a mess, and couldn't stop crying. Mum had died of a heart attack. It was so sudden, and unexpected. I kept seeing her face, and hearing her voice. How could she be dead? I ached for her to hold me, so I could feel her arms around me, smell the talcum powder she used to love. I called all my friends, and Colin, even though it was the middle of the night. They all tried to help, but there was no way off the island. It was awful, knowing Mum was gone and my family were all waiting for me so they could have her funeral.

'Just get me home somehow,' I sobbed. In the end, I had to fly to Gran Canaria, then on to Gatwick. I sobbed for the entire flight, but felt a calmness and strength when I landed.

'Not long now, Mum,' I whispered. 'I'm nearly there.'

Then I froze. It was like a vibration, a soft humming in the air, and I knew it was Star. I'd let my guard down in grief, and she was back. This time, instead of rejecting her, I let her in. She didn't say or do anything. I just felt her, comforting me. I smiled, grateful. I'd turned my back on her years before, but she hadn't abandoned me. She'd been waiting for when I was ready to accept her. I'd been an angry young woman, scared and in pain when I'd raged at her. Now I realized it wasn't her fault. She was with me as I caught a taxi to the chapel of rest. I had to see Mum.

She was beautiful still, but looked tiny. She was five foot six and slim when alive, but now she looked like a little porcelain doll. All her wrinkles had gone, and she was child-like.

'I love you,' I said, kissing her cheek. It was soft but cold, which startled me. This was Mum's body, but she wasn't here. My vibrant, happy mum, who bustled around looking after us all and ignoring her pain wasn't here, in this room. My hot, silent tears fell as I stroked her hair and held her hand that looked so much like mine.

'I miss you,' I whispered, my grief ragged inside. But it was comforting to be here, not macabre. I pulled a rose quartz stone out of my pocket and placed it in her hand. It was my favourite stone, but I wanted Mum to have it, so she always had a little piece of me with her. I sat there, nattering to her for a while, then finally tore myself away. I was exhausted and it was Mum's funeral the next day.

That night I collapsed in bed back at the flat I used to share with Simon, and plunged into a deep sleep. Hours later I woke up to a familiar sight – gold, silver and blue shards of light exploding in the gloom. It was Star, and there was someone with her, smaller, with a baby pink shimmer around her. I stared at the petite shape and gasped. Mum was holding Star's hand.

'I'm OK, love,' she said as I fought not to cry. I wasn't sad, though, I was ecstatic to see Mum again, and she looked so happy. Her face was line-free and the glow around her radiated peace.

'I'm not in pain any more,' she reassured me. 'And I want you to go back to Tenerife. It'll be good for you.'

I was overwhelmed, laughing and crying at once. I knew how lucky I was. Star had given me the most special gift. She'd brought Mum to see me for one last time, and it meant so much to me. She stayed for just five minutes, but I felt Mum's love and it made me stronger.

The next day, I didn't break down at her funeral. I knew Mum was out of pain and happy. And now, because of her visit, I knew what to do. I'd been fighting it for years, but I had a gift that was rare and special. Instead of ignoring it, I was going to develop it, and see what happened.

Back at the house, I rummaged in the chest of drawers in my old bedroom. There, right at the back, under some old books and magazines, I found them – my Tarot cards. I'd put them to one side when I'd turned my back on Star. Now I threw them in my handbag. Somehow I just knew I'd need them where I was going.

4

Witches and willies

The dog looked so forlorn, I couldn't help laughing. He was the ugliest pug I'd ever seen, and the wizard's hat and tiny velvet cloak he was wearing didn't make him look any better. His owner, dressed as a witch, was standing outside the diner as if this was the most natural thing in the world.

'Is this Salem?' I asked. The witch nodded.

'I love your accent,' she grinned. 'What are you doing here?'

It was Hallowe'en, and I'd flown to the United States to do readings at the world-famous psychic fayre that was held annually in the small Massachusetts town. I'd always wanted to go to Salem, a place notorious for the witch trials of 1692, when nineteen men and women were hanged at Gallows Hill after mass hysteria broke out among the residents. The witch hunt is said to have started after a group of teenaged girls faked possession, claiming it was the work of local women, who could fly.

For centuries afterwards, the village was plagued by disaster. Crops failed, businesses collapsed and villagers spoke of hearing and seeing things until they posthumously 'acquitted' the women – a bit late after they'd persecuted, convicted and killed them, but it put the place on the tourist and international Wiccan and psychic map. Several episodes of 'Bewitched', the seventies sitcom about Samantha, the nose-twitching witch, were filmed there, and now it hosted a masked ball every Hallowe'en, to which it was impossible to engineer an invitation.

But I'd got one. A friend of an American guy I'd done a reading for had invited me over to work in a shop called Angelica's. Bizarrely, another friend asked me to do readings at the psychic fayre and attend the masked ball. So, on a whim, I'd said yes and jumped on a plane to Boston. Now, after driving through the sleet for an hour, I was here.

'I'm a clairvoyant,' I told the witch. 'I'm looking for Angelica's.' She pointed up the high street.

'You must come in The Witches Hat,' she said. 'My friend, the owner, would love to meet you.'

I was hungry, and needed to eat. So I promised the witch I'd call round later, and headed to Angelica's. It was shut. 'Great,' I thought, irritated. It had taken me sixteen hours, door to door, to get here. 'You'd have thought they'd be here to meet me,' I muttered.

Spinning round, I crunched back through the snow to the diner. Starving, I tucked into pancakes, maple syrup and bacon, then headed back to see if anyone had turned up at Angelica's. It was still closed. On the way back to my car, I passed the witch, still standing there with her pug.

'Serena really wants to meet you,' she said, so I tagged along after her.

The Witches Hat was a Wiccan boutique, full of spell books, potions and candles. I smiled as I entered. It was like stepping into a shop straight out of a Harry Potter book. By the counter there were wands, medicine balls and gems for sale. Large hanging crystals threw rainbows of light across the store, while the ceiling was a witch's or wizard's dream. Suspended from it were row upon row of broomsticks, and hats in every size. At eye level, ceremonial swords, cloaks and dragon's blood vied with the most gorgeous witch's gowns I'd ever seen. Assistants dressed in dark velvet sprinkled me with fairy dust as I walked in, so the whole place sparkled. It was warm and modern, not musty and cold. And in the middle of the shop were two stools.

'They're for readings,' the witch said. A black drape, hanging from the ceiling like a shower curtain, could be pulled around the stools for privacy.

Serena looked exactly as I'd expected – in her 50s, I guessed, with long, grey hair. She was wearing a long, velvet dress and around her neck was a turquoise crystal as big as a mug.

'It's fantastic to meet you,' she beamed, and I beamed back. Her motherly energy was as big as her necklace, and I warmed to her.

'Why don't you give me a reading?' she suggested. I had time to kill until Angelica's opened, so I perched on one of the stools and pulled out my Tarot cards. She swished the curtain around us, and instantly I could sense someone else was there. As Serena shuffled the cards, I connected with Spirit, and saw the man immediately. He was handsome with long hair, big brown eyes and Mediterranean features.

'Ben's behind you,' I said. 'He passed very recently of a heart attack and says you're going to take a plane very soon.' Serena shook her head.

'No, I know a Ben, but he's not dead,' she said. I stared at Ben. He was persistent.

'He says you're going to get on a plane today and fly five or six hours across America,' I repeated. Serena burst out laughing.

'This is my busiest time of the year,' she said, holding up her hands. Rolling her eyes, she explained that Ben was her husband but they'd split up. 'We're still friends and talk all the time, though,' Serena said. 'So I know he's not dead.'

We carried on like that for ten minutes. Ben was insistent that Serena needed to organize his funeral, and she was equally adamant that she wasn't going anywhere. Eventually, he drew back, and Serena and I agreed to disagree.

'You're so funny,' she said. 'But you've got it all wrong.' She was good-natured about it, and we parted on good terms.

'This is my number,' I said, scribbling it down. 'If Angelica turns up looking for me, can you tell her I've gone back to my hotel?' She nodded, promising to pass on the message.

Back at my room, I took a bath, and lay in it for an hour, letting the hot water ease my joints. I was so relaxed I jumped when the phone rang, sloshing water over the side as I sprang up. It was Serena.

'He's dead,' she said, her voice shrill. I paused, my mind racing to catch up with what she meant.

'Who?' I asked.

'Ben. My son's just called to say he's dead. I've got to fly to California right away.'

She was in shock, and wanted to know if I could work at her

shop while she was gone because it would be so busy. Of course I agreed. It would have been rude to say no, after accidentally telling her within five minutes of meeting her that she was about to become a widow. Normally, I wouldn't predict a death for anyone. It would be too upsetting and morally wrong, but Ben was in Spirit when he gave me the message. I'd blurted it out unaware he'd only just passed over.

'Can you start work now?' Serena asked, her voice cracking. 'I need to get to the airport.'

I agreed and quickly got ready. As I walked back down the high street, I stood out like the proverbial sore thumb. Everyone else was dressed as a witch. I was wearing jeans, a crop top, snow boots and puffa jacket.

'I hardly look the part,' I thought, but then I never did like fancy dress. I was more of a designer labels girl. Well, I was born and brought up in Essex. Even mediums have plenty of bling there!

I'd had leaflets printed to take with me, and I put one in the window of The Witches Hat: 'London's top psychic, Jayne Wallace, available for readings' it declared. Within half an hour there was a queue out of the shop. 'Have you seen that British girl?' everyone was saying, and I could hardly keep up with demand. 'Maybe I should have been in marketing,' I thought, swishing the curtain around another customer. I did reading after reading but the queue didn't seem to get any shorter.

'Can you go and check if Angelica's is open?' I asked the witch. Guilt tore at me. I'd flown over to work there. What would Angelica think if she saw me doing brisk trade here?

'Why did I have to open my big mouth?' I thought, shaking my head. But Angelica's was still shut, the witch reported, so I didn't feel so bad. It was closed the next day, and the day after that, so it was fate that I'd walked into The Witches Hat and passed on Ben's message. What would I have done otherwise? I was so busy, I fell into the bath or bed whenever I went back to my hotel.

On the day of the Hallowe'en masked ball, I had a phone call from back home as I lay on the bed. It was a producer of 'The Graham Norton Show'. I'd done a reading for him a few weeks earlier, but hadn't thought any more of it. Now he was asking if I wanted to appear on the show. A thrill of excitement rushed through me. I loved Graham Norton and had been in the audience a couple of times to watch the programme being filmed. Of course I wanted to appear on his show.

'We need you on this Friday's show,' the producer said, and my heart sank. I wasn't flying home until the following week.

'I'm in America,' I said, trying to hide my disappointment. The producer wasn't having any of it.

'What if we flew you back early?' he said. 'Graham really wants you on and there's a fantastic star guest I bet you'd love to meet.'

I was torn between finishing my trip in Salem or leaving early.

'Let me think about it,' I said. 'Call me tomorrow.' I hung up, irritated. Why did everything always happen at once? I'd deliberately booked myself into this gorgeous bed and breakfast so I could make a holiday out of my trip, and I was loving every minute. But how could I turn down 'The Graham Norton Show'? 'It'll happen if it's meant to,' I told myself.

I found the lure of TV irresistible. I loved the thrill of appearing on camera live – when anything could go wrong. For a psychic, it's raising the stakes because we need spirits to come through to do our job well. I'm lucky in that I always have Star with me, and she's never let me down, but there's always that little doubt at the back of my head, nagging away. As a live show starts, I'll be thinking, 'This could be the first time.'

That's the fear I felt – and pushed away – as I sat opposite TV presenter Kate Silverton when I made my TV debut on 'The Psychic Show'. I'd ended up on the show after my friend Nicola came for a reading and I told her that she was going to do very well on 'Stars In Their Eyes'. She was startled, because she'd only just filled in the application form to go on it.

'You're going to be in the final,' I told her and she squealed.

Sure enough, a couple of weeks later, she auditioned, and was told she was through to the show, which was being filmed in Manchester.

'I'll come and see you,' I told her. I didn't know why I said that. I had no plans to go to Manchester.

Later that day I was watching TV with my boyfriend Leigh when 'The Psychic Show' came on. It was the first time I'd seen it, and I was fascinated, watching mediums do readings using Tarot, psychometry – touching an object to read the owner – and clairvoyancy.

'You should be on that,' Leigh said. Leigh Ryan and I had met years earlier when I'd spotted him on the door of Epping Forest

Country Club in Essex. He had been wearing a dinner jacket and bow tie, standing 6ft tall with a body builder's physique and the bluest eyes.

'You're the best looking man I've seen in years,' I'd said, unusually forward. 'Can I kiss you?' I hadn't waited for an answer and had been shocked to find myself giving a smacker to a gorgeous stranger with the softest lips. He'd taken my number, then taken me out. We have now been together for 14 years.

Leigh saying I should be on 'The Psychic Show' made me think about it. No one was doing crystal readings and I was sure that would make great TV.

'I'm going to see if I can get on there,' I said, waiting for the credits to discover who made the show. It was a production company in Manchester.

'I want to do crystal readings on your show,' I told the woman who answered the phone. She asked me a few questions, then asked me to send my CV. I didn't have one, so Leigh and I spent the afternoon putting one together. It must have worked because the following week they asked me to go up and appear.

'Oh no,' I muttered, hanging up from the producer. 'Leigh, what have I got myself into?'

I'd never been anywhere near a TV studio before and now I was going on live.

'You'll be fine,' Leigh said. 'It's no different from doing an ordinary reading.'

I tried to be brave, but all the way there, and waiting in the green room, my stomach churned. 'Please help me,' I begged Star, but even her reassuring voice in my head didn't stop me trembling.

'What am I doing here?' I thought, fear knotting inside me. My mouth was dry, my mind had gone blank, and my palms were sweating. I thought I'd look like a rabbit in the headlights, sitting opposite Kate, and then I wouldn't be able to speak. Just then a runner appeared.

'Come on through,' she smiled, and I followed her on my wobbly legs.

The reading was simple, just like I do all day every day. The person being read had to choose a crystal, and based on that, I would give them insights into their past, present and future, as well as any messages that came through from Spirit. 'Easy enough,' I told myself, but then I realized that millions of people would be watching the show all over the country.

I gulped as I sat down opposite Kate, and saw the floor manager counting down for filming to start. But then an inner calm descended, and I was able to relax and smile. The reading was a blur, I just let my psychic instinct – and Star – get me through it. At the end, I couldn't stop grinning. I'd done it – and I hadn't mucked up.

'Brilliant,' Kate said, winding up the segment. 'Let's hear it for Jayne Wallace.' The audience were clapping, and I stumbled off stage, relieved.

'You were fantastic,' the producer said. 'Can you come on next week?' I laughed, dazed.

'Really?' I repeated and she nodded. So we arranged for me to come back up to Manchester a few days later, and on the way out I bumped into Nicola.

'I'm through to the final,' she said. 'Just as you told me. You have to come and watch.' It was on the next week – the day I was appearing back on 'The Psychic Show'.

'I'll be there,' I promised, and so I dashed over to her studio as soon as I'd appeared on the programme, and was incredibly proud to watch Nicola singing as Madonna.

I'd been on several shows since then, but Graham Norton was special. Was it worth going back early for? I didn't have time to decide. Right then, I had to get an outfit for the ball. I wandered out into the long high street, already packed with revellers, dressed-up in the most amazing costumes. Fairy lights twinkled in the windows of the Wiccan shops. Witch's outfits in every colour and size were on offer, but I didn't want to dress up in one of them. I've never been drawn to witches, or anything to do with them. I'm more of a spiritual person. I love crystals and cards, not spells. So after window-shopping for an hour, I bought a blue Harry Potter-style hat with a feather in it, and teamed it with a Karen Millen shirt and my new Hugo Boss hipster trousers.

'At least I won't get lost in the crowd,' I thought, slicking on some lipstick and picking up my Tarot cards.

It was a wonderful night. Tickets cost $500 and hundreds of people were there. I set up to give readings in the room above the ballroom, and was busy all night. Word had spread about 'the British girl' and the moment revellers heard my accent they sat down to wait.

'I could get used to this,' I thought, happy I was proving so popular. Once the session finished, I weaved through the partygoers downstairs. Everyone was drinking and dancing and

I drank in the atmosphere. It was one of the most spectacular balls I'd ever been lucky enough to attend, and I didn't fall into bed until the early hours. The producer woke me up.

'We'll fly you business class if you get on the flight tomorrow,' he said over the phone, and I couldn't say no to that.

So the next day I said goodbye to the witch and her pooch, and headed back to Boston airport with all my expenses paid and $3,000 in my pocket. On the Virgin Atlantic flight, I relaxed and enjoyed my complimentary toiletries and extra leg room. 'This is the life,' I thought, wishing I liked champagne. I hardly ever drank – didn't enjoy the taste of alcohol. I made do with a cup of tea and a video, and the time flew by.

A car was waiting to pick me up from the airport and take me home to change and pick up Leigh. 'Are you OK?' I asked him, dashing into the shower. Then it was back into the car and off to the studio. I was so excited, I couldn't stop grinning. This was how celebrities must feel, flying in to the country and heading straight into make-up for a TV show. I glanced at my watch. It was only a couple of hours until I was on. The show's pre-recorded as live, so even though it's filmed in advance, once it starts it keeps going as if it was really on air. Only a disaster would cause the director to shout, 'Cut.'

Luckily, we had a clear run up to town and arrived at the studios on London's embankment in plenty of time.

'Hair, make-up, then rehearsal,' the runner told me, escorting us to my dressing room.

'They're really giving me the VIP treatment,' I giggled to Leigh. They were even organizing a bottle of champagne for us.

'It'll be here when you get back from rehearsal,' the runner said. We followed him down to the set. It looked much smaller than on TV. 'Here's the producer.' The runner handed us over to a young guy with short hair.

'Glad you could make it,' he grinned, walking us into the middle of the set. 'We're going to have a lot of fun tonight.'

I nodded, clasping my hands together. What did they want me to do? Give celebrity readings?

'We want it to be like a game show,' the producer began. A woman was going to sit in the hot seat, while I read three guys' anatomies in special booths, so she couldn't see us. From the anatomy, I had to describe the men's personalities, so she could identify which one was her partner.

'Simple,' I thought. Then I paused. I could feel Leigh bristling beside me.

'What part of their anatomy exactly?' he asked. The producer looked at him, then me, and immediately we both knew what he was suggesting. I stepped back at exactly the same time as Leigh.

'No way,' we both said together. The producer smiled calmly, as if he dealt with this kind of thing all the time.

'It's not a problem,' he said. 'They won't be anywhere near you.' But I was shaking my head.

'Absolutely not. I'm a medium. I don't read body parts,' I said. Leigh was furious, but the producer was talking to some other people backstage.

'What if they were covered up, wearing pants and long shirts?' he suggested.

I didn't have a problem with that. I could see it would be funny, but Leigh wasn't so sure.

'It'll be cheeky, not smutty,' I said, choosing my words carefully. 'You know what Graham's like.'

Leigh and I went backstage, and I chatted on, telling him about my trip, hoping to calm him down. But he was steaming. 'I really don't want you to do it,' he kept saying, but I couldn't cancel now. I'd flown all the way back just to go on the show. It had already started filming. I couldn't let them down.

'It'll be fine,' I told Leigh.

I wasn't on until the last quarter, so we settled back and watched Graham being his usual funny self on the giant TV.

'Look who the other guest is,' I squealed. I was going to be on with Pink, one of my favourite singers. I'd been awake for twenty-two hours now, but excitement swept away my jet lag. Leigh didn't share my enthusiasm. He was still pestering about the readings. I was about to appear on TV with two of my idols. I was too tired to be nervous, and tried to shake myself awake as I was taken backstage to have a microphone and earpiece put on me.

'Ready?' the producer said and I nodded.

Leigh squeezed my hand, but I could tell he was still annoyed. I closed my eyes for a split second and focused, calling on Star to help me. Then I heard my name being called and stepped out on set. It was surreal shaking hands with Graham and smiling at Pink. And then it was time to play the game.

Graham led me into a tiny booth they'd built especially for the readings. I had to sit down while the man stood to the side of me. 'Contestant number one,' Graham announced and instantly I started describing him. But I was getting the information from his aura, definitely not from his privates.

'And now contestant number two,' Graham said, leading me into the next booth. The same thing happened. His aura was easy to read, and Pink was making everyone laugh by writing some of the words I was saying on a board to make cheeky sentences.

Finally, it was time to do the same with contestant number three. As soon as I sat down, he pretended to thrust at me. He was just playing around and trying to get a laugh from the audience. But I instinctively put my hands up and pushed him back. He stumbled backwards, making the booth wobble.

'Stop filming,' I said, shocked, 'I'm not doing this.' I stared at the guy, who was looking shame-faced. 'How dare you?' I ranted. 'What do you think you're doing, thrusting in my face.'

Graham rushed over, and put his arm around me. I was up for a joke, but that guy had gone over the limit. Luckily, Leigh was still backstage, and Pink was giving the guy a telling off.

'Are you OK?' Graham asked and I nodded. The guy apologized, and I agreed to finish filming.

'Which one is your boyfriend?' Graham asked the girl at the end. She correctly told him, 'Number two.'

It was a laugh, except for that glitch, but Leigh wasn't in the best of moods. 'It's OK,' I kept telling him. It was fun, but I've never done an anatomy reading since. I've stuck to my Tarot cards and mediumship. I didn't want to be known as the clairvoyant who read privates, even if it was all in the best possible taste.

5

'I should be so lucky'

Tearing open the envelope, I sighed. It was a red gas bill for £120 and I didn't have the money. I was 22, had a stall at Camden Market, did readings at psychic fayres and was officially skint. Just then the phone rang.

'Let's go to bingo,' my sister Julie said. 'It'll be a laugh.'

I needed cheering up, but there was no way I was going to waste money I didn't have on bingo.

'Sorry, I'm broke,' I told her. 'And any money I do have has got to go on bills.' But she wasn't having any of it.

'I'll shout you a game,' she insisted. 'Come on, it'll be fun.'

She wouldn't take no for an answer so eventually I gave in. I'd never played before, but it was a night out, and an excuse to dress up. My friend Michelle was coming too, and she was a bingo fanatic. She went without fail every week, and took it very seriously.

'I've got some special pens for us to play with,' she said when I arrived at the bingo hall in Ilford. I tried not to laugh as she fanned them out. 'They're my bingo pens.'

She was looking at me expectantly. I chose a purple one.

'I feel lucky,' I said, following them in.

The hall was already crowded, and we had to find a table at

the back. Michelle was a bit cross because she liked to sit in the same place every time, but someone else had already nabbed it.

'It's not going to be my night now,' she grumbled, laying all her bingo paraphernalia out on the table.

'What do I have to do?' I asked, gazing around at the women packed into the hall, and feeling their excitement. Michelle leant forward.

'Just cross off the numbers on your card when they're called out,' she said. 'You get money for a line. And shout house if you get every number.'

I nodded. I was a bingo virgin, but even I could remember that. Julie ordered us some drinks and paid £20 for my ticket. 'Blimey, that's a lot,' I thought. I'd imagined it would be a couple of pounds, but that explained the nervous energy in the room.

'Eyes down, ladies,' a wannabe TV host in a waistcoat announced, and the room went quiet. I watched the balls being picked, and crossed off my numbers as they were called. Julie kept smiling across at me, but Michelle was too engrossed to look up from her card. I had a few numbers crossed off now and could feel excitement rising along with my lemonade bubbles.

'Unlucky for some,' the caller said, and I crossed off thirteen. 'Two fat ladies,' he said next and I had to look at Michelle, confused. He was talking another language.

'What number's that?' I whispered. She didn't even lift her eyes.

'Eighty-eight,' she hissed back and up I jumped.

'House,' I shrieked. 'Over here, house!'

Julie clapped her hands together, while Michelle grabbed my

card. An assistant was heading over to check my numbers but Michelle was shaking her head.

'You don't have all of them,' she said under her breath to me, and to the assistant, 'Sorry, there's been a mistake.' Her cheeks were flushed, and guilt tore through me. I'd embarrassed her in front of all her bingo cronies.

'It's my first time,' I told the caller. 'I got a bit too excited.'

All the women round about were tutting and rolling their eyes, but I hadn't meant to get it wrong. I'd just got carried away. Luckily, they soon forgot about me when the caller started again. This time I just glanced down at my card.

'Key to the door, number eighteen,' he said, and I crossed it off. I needed one more. 'Number two,' the caller said next, and I laughed. I had it.

'Michelle,' I said, thrusting my card across the table. 'Check it. I think I really do have full house now.' Sighing, she took it off me and double-checked all the number. Then she looked up and nodded. I raised my eyebrows and she smiled.

'Shout it then,' she said and I yelled, 'House.' A few people groaned when they saw it was me. But when the caller checked my card, she confirmed it. I'd won.

'What do I get?' I asked. I'd won £140 cash – exactly the amount I needed to pay Julie back my stake and the gas bill.

'Lucky so and so,' I heard one woman mutter, and she was right.

I'd always been lucky. I don't know if it was Star all along, helping me, fate or my own lucky aura but whenever I needed something I always got it, no matter how ridiculous. One time, I was standing in a queue at Los Angeles airport. I'd been to see a TV producer with my friend Ali, who worked in TV. We'd had a brilliant time but I was dreading the long, boring flight home. Ali and I were in the check-in queue, which was moving at a snail's pace, and I was amusing myself by scrutinizing the first-class passengers, who were also checking-in.

'Look at that luggage,' I said to Ali, pointing to the biggest pile of Louis Vuitton suitcases I'd ever seen. One, the size of a small wardrobe, cost £15,000. I knew that because I'd seen it on TV – and this guy had the entire collection. 'They're probably worth more than my house.'

We glanced down at our little suitcases. A few hours ago I'd thought they looked smart but now they seemed shabby compared with the designer luggage. Just then I heard Star's voice.

'I'm going to get an upgrade,' I announced, smoothing down my shirt. Ali rolled her eyes.

'Yeah, right, and I'm going to marry the pilot,' she said. I smiled at her.

'I'm flying home first class. Just wait and see,' I told her.

Star was never wrong and I was feeling very, very lucky. Just then I heard a man laughing in the first-class queue to the side of me. I glanced over and caught his eye.

'Want to swap places?' I asked, never backward in coming forward. The guy shook his head, but started talking.

'Where are you girls going?' he asked in a booming American accent.

'London,' I said, pointing to the check-in desk sign. 'Only

we're in the back of the plane and you're in the front.'

He was friendly and told us that he was with a group of singers and musicians going to play for Sony Music in London.

'Are you famous then?' I asked, peering at him. He didn't look familiar but one of the guys in the background looked just like Snoop Doggy Dog. 'Is that who I think it is?' I went on, and the man nodded.

'Yes, and I'm Spliff,' he said. 'And that is Busta Rhymes.'

There was a pause as if he expected us to be impressed. I shrugged, and so did Ali.

'Never heard of him,' I said.

'Do you recognize this?' he said and began to sing 'Baby, if you give it to me, I'll give it to you' and straightaway, I began humming along. The song, 'Give It To Me', had been a hit for Busta, featuring Mariah Carey.

'So that's how he can afford so much Louis Vuitton,' I exclaimed. We'd reached the front of our queue now.

'See you later, ladies,' Spliff drawled as we began the process of checking in and he and his party were whisked through first-class. I watched them go, then handed my passport and economy ticket to the Virgin Atlantic check-in girl, waiting for her to offer me my upgrade. Nothing. I smiled so much my cheeks began to ache. Still no offer. Ali started to giggle.

'There you go,' the check-in clerk said, handing me my economy boarding card.

'You just wait,' I hissed to Ali, who couldn't stop laughing as we went through customs.

Finally, we made it into the duty free, and I hurried to buy some presents for Leigh and my family before we were called to our gate. Looking around, I couldn't see Busta, Snoop or Spliff. 'They'll be in the first-class lounge,' I thought. 'Where I should be.' It didn't make sense. Star never told me anything that didn't happen. And I didn't know how I was going to sit next to Ali all the way home with her sniggering all the time.

'OK, so I got it wrong,' I sighed as she laughed again.

Just then the Tannoy crackled, startling me, and a tinny voice intoned, 'Could Miss Jayne Wallace come to the reservations desk?'

'Yes,' I cried, jumping up and hurrying off. I arrived out of breath, so eager was I to find out what they wanted.

'We've upgraded your ticket, madam,' the woman at the desk said. I didn't know how, why or who, but ten seconds later I was holding a first-class ticket in my hand. Of course, I felt bad about Ali.

'We'll share it,' I suggested. 'I'll do the first half, then we'll swap.' She grinned, equally excited.

It was the first time I'd turned left on an aeroplane and I had to force myself not to squeal when I saw my bed and the bar, with champagne on ice, in the cabin. After rummaging through the goody bag supplied, and examining the complimentary toiletries and pyjamas, I looked across at my neighbour. It was Spliff.

'Hi again,' he said, shaking my hand. We didn't stop talking as we took off.

'What do you do?' he asked and whistled when I told him I was a clairvoyant.

'Wow! Can you do me a reading?' he asked. So 33,000 feet up in the air, I found myself shuffling my Tarot cards and telling him all about his career and love life. Busta came over and shook his head.

'I don't believe in that stuff,' he said, when Spliff urged him to have a reading. Just then I had a powerful image of something dramatic that had happened in his past. I knew he wouldn't want me to say it out loud, and guessed it was something he'd never spoken about. So I leant forward and whispered it in his ear. He looked shocked.

'OK, give me a reading,' he said, sitting down. He was easy to read, the messages came through so clearly, even though we were in midair.

'I'll drink to that,' he said afterwards, pouring us both a large glass of champagne. Normally, I don't drink but it's not often you find yourself in first class over the Atlantic, hanging out with one of the world's most famous rappers, so I made an exception. Ali's jaw dropped when she came down to see me, sitting between Busta and Spliff, sipping Moet.

'You're a jammy cow,' she informed me as Spliff poured her a glass and we toasted my good luck.

Fate always comes to my aid whenever I need something – or thinks I deserve it.

So many holidays with Leigh have become really amazing because I always end up giving readings to people I meet. One time, Leigh and I saved up all our money to go on a holiday of a lifetime. We flew to Bermuda, planning to stay there for a week, then cruise around the Caribbean on a luxury ship.

I couldn't wait, and loved the island the moment we arrived. I'd been working hard and my rheumatoid arthritis had been particularly bad, but in the heat, the gnawing pain in my joints subsided to a dull ache.

'Wouldn't it be amazing to stay here for ages?' I said to Leigh, as we lazed on sunloungers by the pool. He nodded, stretching out to catch even more of the sun.

We had everything we needed – a luxury hotel by a sandy beach that was lapped by a clear blue sea. But we had to be careful – we didn't have lots of money to splash around. We'd managed to save up for the trip, but were on a limited budget. I flicked through what was on offer at the hotel as I sunbathed, and smiled when I saw they did liquorice tea at the spa. That was my favourite, and now I had to have one. 'Wish I could afford a massage, too,' I thought, but that was impossible. Besides, I was already relaxing, laying in the sun, so a tea would be more than enough.

'Back in a minute,' I said to Leigh, who thought it was funny I was prepared to give up precious sunbathing minutes to fetch a drink. The spa was cool compared with outside.

'May I have a liquorice tea, please?' I said to the beautician at the desk. She had been reading a magazine but quickly closed it, putting it down as she looked up quizzically at me. I smiled, a little uncomfortable. She continued to stare and I wondered if I had a giant spot on the end of my nose that I didn't know about.

'I don't believe it,' she said at last, picking up her magazine. All was explained. She was holding a copy of *Spirit & Destiny* – and the page was open at the column I wrote for them every month. 'I absolutely love you' she said.

My cheeks would have gone red if I wasn't pink from the sun already.

'Thanks,' I grinned. 'May I have a liquorice tea?'

Her name was Sara, and we chatted while she made the tea. She asked if I'd give her a reading.

'I can trade if you like,' she said. 'You give me a reading and I'll give you a massage.' I didn't need asking twice.

'Done,' I said. So after I'd finished my tea, I did her reading, which was mostly about her relationships and work, and she seemed more than happy.

'I'm sure the other girls would love a reading, too,' she said as she massaged my aching body. And they did. So every day, while Leigh topped up his tan, I'd do readings for the girls in the spa, then have facials and beauty treatments in exchange.

'I've never looked as glam in my life,' I told them.

I became close to the spa director, Louise, over the holiday, and since she knew many of the staff on the ship we were going on next, she mentioned me to them.

'They said they'd like readings,' she said. 'And they'll trade.' She also suggested holding a psychic school on the island six months later. 'I'll help organize it,' she offered. 'Everyone will want to come once they know who you are.' I told her I'd think about it. I had to be able to pay for my flights and hotel while I taught the school.

Louise must have really spread the word, because I was greeted like a celebrity when Leigh and I joined the ship.

'Everyone wants a reading,' one of Louise's friends, who

worked in the spa on board, told me. 'And the tourists are happy to pay cash.'

So I did a couple of hours of readings every day, and made enough cash to fund coming back for the psychic school. When I went back six months later, Louise had booked teachers, doctors and businessmen and women from all over the world. One man flew over especially from Japan while a woman jetted in from New York.

'I told them you're the best,' Louise said. She was amazing and should have set up her own business, running events. Louise joined the class, and made sure I was treated like a VIP, with more beauty treatments than I'd ever had in my life back home, a beautiful hotel room and delicious food.

I imagined that's what life would be like if I won the lottery. I have tried to win, but I've only ever managed a tenner. I don't know if it's Star's way of making sure I appreciate the meaning of money, but I've never been able to predict the winning numbers for myself. I suppose that's only right, otherwise where would you draw the line? How would you ever think enough is enough? Now, working for a living, I still appreciate lovely things and I'm so lucky that people are very generous and give me presents.

One of my regular clients, Fi Hinchclif, came to see me for a reading last winter, holding the most gorgeous Jimmy Choo handbag – chocolate brown leather with fur trim.

'That's gorgeous,' I said, stroking it. After I'd done her reading, she emptied it and handed it over.

'For you,' she smiled. 'You deserve it.' I told her not to be silly, but she refused to take no for an answer. I couldn't believe her generosity and I've used that handbag during every cold spell since. It's one of my favourite things and always reminds me of her.

Another client who spoils me is a wealthy woman who lives in Dubai and loves horse racing. One time, she rang my mobile from a very big race meeting, asking me to name all of the horses that were going to win, so she could bet on them.

'I have absolutely no idea,' I laughed, hearing all her friends having a good time in the background. But she kept asking, so I suggested she read out the names of the horses. As soon as she said the name Red Velvet, I knew it was the winner. She placed a wedge of money on it and rang back excitedly half an hour later to say it had won. I correctly predicted the rest of the day's winners for her and she made a small fortune, impressing her friends.

'She's my lucky mascot,' I heard her say, which made me smile.

A few days later a parcel arrived in the post. Inside was a Gucci watch. 'Thank you' the note from my friend read. A box of chocolates or bunch of flowers would have been more than enough, but I was made up. Now I call it my lucky watch, and wear it whenever I want something good to happen. It's never let me down so far.

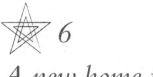

6

A new home for Psychic Sisters

The view from the window was not enticing. Grey clouds hovered over even greyer streets, and sleet was falling. Dirty, days-old snow lay in piles that refused to melt. Why was I going out in this? Because I was stubborn.

It was January, and my friend Christine had suggested meeting for lunch since she was working in London, so I called her and arranged it.

'Can you give me a reading?' she asked. That didn't bother me. Doing a reading was like breathing for me, it was so natural. So I picked up my Tarot cards and off I went. Christine was always good company. Lunch would be fun, but we couldn't be too long because she was on air later that afternoon. She was a clairvoyant, too, and worked on psychic TV shows.

Whilst we were in town, I asked Christine if she'd mind coming with me to Selfridges on Oxford Street. A few days earlier I'd treated Leigh and myself to some of my favourite Aveda beauty products in the sale but they'd accidentally forgotten to put the foot gel I'd bought into the bag so I wanted to go and collect it. I thought it would be quiet because of the sleet, but Selfridges was packed. We had to fight our way through the crowds of sales shoppers to reach the Aveda counter. They gave me my missing foot gel, and we headed to the nearby café.

'I'll do your cards when we sit down,' I told Christine, but there weren't any tables. The café was full. I looked at the waiter and he shrugged. Just then Star told me to go round again.

'There'll be a table,' she said.

'Let's go round,' I told Christine, who trailed behind me. We circled the café and as we arrived back where we started, there was a table for two right in front of us. Result!

I waited for the waiter to clear the table, then began laying out my Tarot cards in a Celtic Cross spread. Christine wanted to know as much as possible, so I needed to study a general spread of cards, showing her past, present and future. Sipping my cappuccino, I focused, and so was quiet for once. Then I began reading Christine's cards.

For me, the messages, signs and meanings come so fast I don't have time to stop and think about them. They tumble out of my mouth in a rush, and I have to race to keep up. I don't want to miss anything, so I let it all out in a stream of consciousness, spouting off names, and any tiny detail I'm given. Sometimes I don't even know what it means, but I pass it on anyway. It always seems to make sense to the person I'm reading for, and the tiniest detail, which is meaningless to me, has some deep significance for them.

Today, Christine nodded and asked questions, as I read and passed on what I knew. While I worked, out of the corner of my eye, I noticed a man staring at us. He was standing on the other side of the café, watching intently. The man was very tall, with grey hair, and dressed in a dark grey suit. Beside him, a smart woman was following his gaze. I tried to forget about him, but I could feel his eyes on me. What did he want? Just then I heard Star tell me that this was an important man I needed to speak to, and he was the man that would give me my own shop.

Before I could tell Christine, the man started strolling over, followed by the woman. He came straight up to us.

'What are you up to?' he asked. He was Irish and his eyes were shining even though his face looked serious.

'I'm a clairvoyant and I'm giving her a reading,' I said.

'I don't believe in all that,' he said, shaking his head.

'Well, don't knock it until you try it,' I responded. 'Have you ever had a reading?'

The man shook his head, with a look of utter disbelief on his face at the very idea. As I looked up at him, I felt a message come through for him, so emotional and heartfelt, and I knew it would make a difference to both our lives. I knew I had to pass it on. I jumped up, grabbed his arm and pulled him towards me. Before he could pull away, I whispered the message in his ear, and I could see he was welling up.

'Can you do readings anywhere?'

'Yes,' I said.

'When can you start?' he asked. I was completely taken aback. Addressing his companion, who had been standing back during this exchange, he said, 'I want her in the store.'

'I'm Paul Kelly, managing director of Selfridges,' he said to me, 'and I want you to come and work here.' I laughed.

'Doing what?' I did personal readings, appeared on TV, radio or at psychic fayres. I wasn't a sales assistant. But Paul wanted me to open my own business in Selfridges. It would be the first psychic concession in a department store in the world. I blinked, stunned. Run my own concession?

'I don't know,' I told him. 'I'm a clairvoyant, not a businesswoman.' But Paul Kelly was smiling.

'Please give the Head Buyer of Home your details and I hope to see you soon,' he said, and, shaking my hand, he walked off, leaving me staring open-mouthed at his companion. Her name was Dawn Rose. She explained, in a hushed tone, how the MD never invited people to join Selfridges. What were the chances of that? We'd been in the right place at exactly the right time and had caught his eye.

'He's offering you an amazing opportunity,' she said.

Of course, she was right, and maybe it was fate. Star had told me to go round again to get a table in the café at the exact moment Paul Kelly had been walking past on a store inspection. I'd only come here to pick up a £5 missing foot gel. Maybe this was what I was supposed to do, but I wasn't sure that I could. I didn't know anything about business.

'Let me think about it, but I don't think so,' I said. She took my number anyway, and then we left. Christine headed off to her TV show and I went home. As I handed Leigh his foot gel, I told him what had happened.

'Can you believe it?' I said, laughing. 'I don't have the first clue what to do.'

'You'll figure it out,' Leigh said, smiling. 'You always do.'

We couldn't think about anything else all evening, and the more we talked about it, the more it made sense.

'It's destiny,' I agreed, and rang Christine to ask if she'd come in with me.

'Why not?' she said, and I decided to do it. How hard could it be? I'd had a shop before with Leigh and that had done well so I had some business experience. This was not that different, I told myself. It was just like owning a shop, that was all. And it wasn't like we needed to spend a fortune to set it all up.

'We don't need much,' I told Christine. Our shopping list was small – a mobile phone to take bookings for readings, and some stock to sell, including candles, crystals, dream catchers, incense and smudge sticks, and Tarot cards. I set up a meeting later that week with Paul's assistant Dawn, and it all sounded amazing. The biggest problem was the time scale. Selfridges wanted us ready to start within two months.

'That's crazy,' I gulped. It would take just an hour or so to buy a phone and stock, but we needed staff to do readings – we couldn't work 24/7, and we still needed a name.

Luckily, I'd been a psychic and on the 'circuit' for so long I knew a lot of talented people, so I drew up a shortlist. I wanted a friend, Carolyn, on reception, medium Lindy and clairvoyant, palmist and close friend Robin Lown on the team. They all agreed. Now all we needed was a name. Leigh was in the car one day and blurted out 'What about Psychic Sisters?'

'I love it,' I said, and began organizing T-shirts, leaflets and a giant banner. Although we had Robin with us, we were mainly women, and it had a nice ring to it. It sounded warm, like a family. We all joked with Robin that he would have to dress up like a woman now that he was an official 'sister'. Everyone was so excited, and Leigh gave me lots of support, as well as my friends Vicky Warner, Terri Pearch and Vicky Anderson who owned a local shop in Essex, where I used to rent a room to give readings.

'Where are we going to be?' I asked Dawn and blinked when she told me. Our concession in Selfridges was in the basement, right next to the café where Paul Kelly had spotted us. 'Star knew,' I realized. So it was destiny.

That knowledge gave me the extra energy to push harder to get everything ready. We'd bought the stock and announced we were coming, so we had bookings coming in, but we didn't have any money to dress our space.

'We just need somewhere to sit and a table for the Tarot cards,' I told myself, trying to stop worrying. 'It'll be OK.'

Two days before we were due to open, I was woken in the early hours of the morning by severe shooting pains in my legs. At first, it felt like cramp, but the spasms grew stronger and stronger until my legs were jumping.

'What's going on?' I mumbled, pulling the duvet tighter round myself. My left leg was kicking out, the spasms were so severe, and my heart was now jumping around in my chest. I was shaking, and trying not to cry. My back had started to hurt, and the pain became so bad I had to clench my teeth together to stop myself from screaming.

It happened so quickly. Stumbling out of bed, I grabbed my pain killers. I always had some for my arthritis, but I began to get scared when it didn't even touch the pain. I tried to call Leigh who was at work, but there was no answer. Sobbing, I called an ambulance, and was in a right state when I arrived at Whipps Cross Hospital in Leytonstone. My legs were still jerking and my hands and feet were numb from pins and needles. Test after test was carried out, and a specialist neurologist was called. When I saw my sister Lorraine and Leigh finally arrive, fear twisted in my stomach.

'They think I have a brain tumour,' I told them. The pain was unbelieveable, but I knew the cause was much less serious – a trapped nerve. I'd tried to tell this to the neurologist, but he wasn't convinced and was going to arrange a brain scan.

I had to fight against a panic attack when I was shut into the tiny chamber, but results were inconclusive because I'd had so many hair extensions. It looked like 500 tiny bullets all over my head.

'Why do I have to be so vain?' I chastised myself when the specialist told me the extensions would have to be removed. My hair was too short for my taste, so I'd had extensions put in with copper clips to bulk it up. Now they all had to come out, so the doctors could get a proper look at my brain.

'I know I haven't got a tumour,' I told Leigh and my sister, who both looked dreadful. It was 6am on a Tuesday – two days before the Psychic Sisters concession was due to open in Selfridges. A van had been booked to collect the stock, but who would drive it now? We'd bought a small table and some chairs, and had a bookcase to act as a screen for extra privacy during readings. They had to be taken to the shop. It was so frustrating as there was so much to do before our not-so-grand opening. The entire concession needed putting together, and instead, I was having to drag myself out of hospital to my hairdresser so she could take out all my extensions. It was so frustrating.

'Don't worry, we'll get the shop ready,' the girls promised. I was too weak to argue. I just wanted to feel better, and for the spasms and pain to stop.

While the hairdresser removed my extensions, I stared at my reflection in the mirror and realized that I looked too healthy to have a brain tumour. I didn't look seriously ill. 'Maybe it's just nerves,' I thought, bewildered. I wasn't usually a stress-head, but then this concession was a big deal to me now, and I'd never done anything like it before.

But there was nothing I could do. I was going for a brain scan at 9am, and the girls had to get all the stock in by that time – it had to be done before the store opened to the public. Time ticked by. Finally, the phone rang – the girls had done it. 'Yes,' I thought, hanging up. Then the phone rang again. It was Christine.

'I'm sorry, Jayne, but I can't do it,' she said. What was she talking about? Quietly, she explained she'd had second thoughts about the concession and didn't want to be part of it any more. Christine had her reasons and I understood but given the state I was in, the news went down badly. 'Great!' I muttered. What else could go wrong today?

I was fighting not to panic as I was taken down for the scan, but I was worrying about the store, not any possible tumour. I just wanted to be in Selfridges, helping to set it all up. My consultant and his team came to see me later, and my stomach lurched as they approached. Was it bad news after all? But the neurologist said the brain scan was all clear, and my rheumatologist was smiling. There was no bad news.

'We think you've pushed a disc in your back out of place and that's what caused all the spasms,' a doctor explained. I needed physio to manipulate it back into place, and was discharged the next day. Both Leigh and I went straight to Selfridges. The girls had done a brilliant job. Our Psychic Sisters banner hung above our space.

'What are you doing here?' they asked, their faces worried. I grinned, proud of what they'd achieved.

'I wouldn't miss this for anything,' I said.

We were the first psychic concession ever to open in a department store anywhere in the world. Now all we needed was our first customer.

7

Calamity Jayne

Deep in thought, I didn't hear the woman at first. She could have been standing there for a minute or an hour. I didn't know, I was so absorbed in my own little world.

'Excuse me,' she said, giving a polite cough, and I glanced up. A beautiful woman was smiling down at me. 'I'm here for a reading with Jayne Wallace,' she said in an American drawl.

She looked amazing. Her face was flawless and her skin literally shone with vitality. She was slim, dressed in jeans and a pashmina, and although the effect was casual, each item probably bore a designer label and was undoubtedly very expensive. Effortlessly sophisticated, she was generating quite a bit of attention. I could see both men and women clocking her as they walked past Psychic Sisters in Selfridges, but she was oblivious to it – and that made me like her instantly. She had a nice energy about her, and a spiritual, pure aura.

'Hi,' I grinned. 'Sorry, I was miles away. What was your name again?'

'Belinda,' she answered, following me through to the curtained-off 'booth' section for a reading. We sat opposite each other at a small table.

'Shuffle the cards,' I said, handing her the Tarot pack, but she was easy to read. I'd already connected with Star and was being bombarded with messages.

'I can see you writing a book,' I said, and she nodded. 'I feel that it's an autobiography.' It was weird. Even though I could see her writing, I knew that wasn't her only creative outlet. 'Your career is going through a lot of changes,' I said. 'And your voice is very important, but right now the writing's taking priority.'

There was so much to tell her. She had a busy future, keeping up with all the projects I could see for her, but I could see changes in her life, too.

'You're going on a spiritual journey,' I warned, telling her what pitfalls lay ahead, and how to avoid them. The woman smiled, and seemed happy with what I'd told her.

'Thanks so much,' she said, shaking my hand at the end of the reading, and heading off. I was about to grab a coffee when Michael the floor manager, rushed over.

'Do you know who that was?' he said, excitedly. I shook my head. I didn't have a clue. 'Belinda Carlisle,' he announced, pretending to fan himself. 'I love her.'

'So did I,' I exclaimed, remembering dancing to her hit 'Heaven is a Place on Earth' in the 1980s. How could I fail to recognize her? Now I thought about it, she looked practically the same. 'How embarrassing,' I thought. I'd been so distracted I hadn't really thought too deeply about her. The reading made more sense now, though, especially the vocal symbols that kept coming through. 'Oh well, another celebrity I failed to spot.'

I doubted I'd ever see her again, so I was a little surprised to spot her walking towards me a few months later.

'Everything you told me came true,' she said. 'So I had to come back.'

I gave her another reading, and realized we had a friend in common — Rose, a physiotherapist in Los Angeles. Rose treats a lot of celebrities, and Belinda was one of her clients. She'd recommended me when Belinda had mentioned she was coming to England and wanted a reading. Rose had even rung me to say she had a friend coming and to look after her. What she'd forgotten to mention was that her friend was a global, award-winning pop star. Not that it would have made much difference. I would have treated Belinda as I do anyone else, even if I had been told she was coming.

'I've written my life story, just like you said,' Belinda told me. In fact, her autobiography, *Lips Unsealed*, went on to be a best-seller, as I predicted it would.

'You're going to be here for a while,' I told her, and she nodded.

'That's why you have to give me your phone number,' Belinda said. 'Then we can meet up.'

I hesitated. I rarely gave my number out. It wasn't that I didn't want to speak to Belinda, but after work I was so tired, I always switched off the mobile. And I'd learnt early on that having my number was too much of a temptation for some people. They'd text or ring me at all hours, demanding to know if they were going to get married, win the lottery or have a baby, and such like. But Belinda was different. I really liked her, although I barely knew her.

'I'd rather not,' I told Belinda, apologetically. 'Can I take yours instead? I know it's really cheeky and you should be saying this to me.'

Luckily, Belinda saw the funny side, and happily gave me her number, and in time I gave her mine.

'Now I know we're real friends,' she teased.

One day, Belinda invited Leigh and me and three of her close friends to dinner at a smart restaurant in Belgravia, but although the place was fancy, they were all ordinary people, like us. Belinda looked twenty years younger than her age, and was so down-to-earth, talking about everyday stuff. It was hard to believe she was a global star and performed in front of thousands of people. I didn't see her for a while after that, but she always kept in touch, and would phone as soon as she knew she was flying to the UK.

'I'm in "Hairspray", at the Shaftesbury Theatre,' she said the next time she came to see me. 'You must come and watch.' I was excited about Belinda appearing on the London stage – even more so when she promised to get us tickets. A few weeks later she rang to say she'd arranged for three to be left at the box office. One of the clairvoyants who worked with me, Jackie, was a massive fan and squealed when I invited her. Leigh didn't want to come, but I knew exactly who else to invite – botox Kira, my beautician friend who did everyone's botox, including mine.

Once a year I had some botox to stop my forehead wrinkling when I frowned and to stop the crow's feet appearing at the corners of my eyes. Kira was the best in the country, and we'd become close friends. She was also a massive fan of Belinda's.

'Are you serious?' she shrieked when I rang to tell her. 'I'm on my way.'

I wanted to return the favour for Belinda. She was staying in an apartment that was owned by the theatre, near Shaftesbury Avenue, and there was an uncomfortable atmosphere. She wanted it to feel more homely.

'Will you smudge it for me?' she asked. I was surprised.

'Sure, but how do you know about smudging?' I wanted to know. This is when you cleanse a place of negative energy using a smudge stick, which is made of natural sage leaves bound into a stick. When you light it, the smoke from the embers, along with selected feathers and crystals, disperses the negative energy. The process is a Native American cleansing ritual, which I've performed a lot and always works.

'Great,' Belinda said.

This was the plan – Kira was coming to meet me in the store, Belinda was dropping in her keys, I'd smudge the apartment after work and Kira would help, and then we'd go to the theatre to meet Jackie and watch 'Hairspray'. Easy!

I gathered everything together – the smudge stick, a brown eagle's feather, a large natural smoky quartz crystal, used for grounding and stability, and a small tiger's eye crystal for protection.

'Hold on to these,' I said to Kira when we were ready to go, handing her the apartment keys and the code to get into the building. But when we arrived, the code didn't work.

'I'm sure I wrote it down right,' I muttered, keying in the combination again. The door remained resolutely closed.

'What are we going to do?' Kira said, but I wasn't worried.

I was already buzzing all of the neighbouring apartments.

'Yes?' a voice crackled over the Tannoy, and kindly let us in when we explained we were locked out. We found Belinda's flat easily enough.

'At least we know we've got the right front-door key,' I said, sliding it in the lock. I turned it to the right. Nothing. The door didn't open. I tried it again, and again.

'Let me have a go,' Kira said, jiggling the keys this way and that, but she couldn't get the door to budge either. We looked at each other and began to giggle. This was supposed to be so easy, and it was all going horribly wrong.

'I don't believe this,' Kira sniggered, and we collapsed into fits. A woman in the next apartment must have heard us because she came out.

'Can I help you?' she asked in a very posh voice.

Between giggles, we explained that we were having trouble getting into the apartment and she told us that the key had to go the opposite way from usual – to the left instead of to the right. I turned the key that way, and the door clicked open. Finally, we fell into the flat, and froze. It was gorgeous, like something out of an interiors magazine. The solid oak doors contrasted against the white marble floors. The walls were cream, beige and taupe, and the sofas were so squashy they looked just like giant marshmallows. But Belinda was right. There was a heavy atmosphere that didn't match the sumptuous surroundings.

'Right, let's get on with it,' I said, glancing at my watch. All the shenanigans trying to get into the flat meant we were running late. We had to be at the theatre for 6pm. I set out the crystals, grabbed the feather, went to light the smudge stick and realized that I'd forgotten the matches. Neither of us smoked. 'No,' I muttered. 'What else can go wrong today?' We hunted around and finally found a box of matches.

'Hold this while I light it,' I instructed Kira, handing her the smudge stick.

I'd opened all the windows to let out the smoke, along with negative energy, but the wind blew back in, scattering black cinders from the smudge stick all over the pristine white floor.

'It might leave marks,' I said, rubbing frantically at the black cinders with the sleeve of my T-shirt. The cinders smudged. 'Probably, that's why it's called a smudge stick,' I muttered, beginning to panic.

Embers were flying everywhere and I was scared the white soft furnishings were going to be peppered with tiny burn holes. This was meant to be a favour for a friend but was rapidly turning into a nightmare.

'Get something to cover the smudge stick,' I yelled to Kira. She came rushing back with a saucer, which stopped the red-hot embers scattering all over the coffee and cappuccino-coloured open plan living room.

She began scrubbing the smudge marks off the tiles, while I tried to calm down. The negative energy was going, but now the flat was full of smoke, which Kira and I were breathing in. We would stink of sage when we turned up at the theatre.

'As long as we don't have smoke-dried faces we'll be fine,' I said. It took as long for us to clean up as it did for us to cleanse and energize the apartment, but finally, relieved, we were ready to go.

'Let's hurry,' I said, grabbing our stuff and off we rushed.

Standing outside the theatre, seeing Belinda's name in lights, I couldn't stop grinning.

'Wow!' I said. Then I caught a glimpse of my reflection in a shop window. 'Look at the state of me!' But I hadn't brought any clothes to change into so that was that – my smoky Psychic Sisters T-shirt and jeans would have to do. Kira was checking her reflection, too.

'It doesn't matter,' I said. 'No one will notice us. We'll probably be sat in the stalls, or right at the back.'

But when we met Jackie and gave our names at the box office, they smiled and made a phone call.

'You're in the royal box, Miss Wallace,' the woman said. 'My colleague will show you the way.' Just then a young man arrived.

'Follow me,' he said. 'Miss Carlisle is very excited that you're coming to watch her. She's told me to take good care of you.'

I cringed, pulling my jacket around me. I couldn't have looked – or smelt – worse, and we were going to be in full view of the entire audience as well as the cast.

'Can I get you anything?' the man asked, opening the door leading in to the royal box. We all shook our heads in unison. Truth was we'd bought chocolates and cans of cola on the way. I hid the bag of goodies under my chair until the lights dimmed, then happily scoffed my favourite Minstrels and Maltesers while watching the play.

Belinda was amazing but unrecognizable. Her usually glossy hair was platinum blonde and giant, and her outfits were just as huge. Her voice was still the same as it was twenty years ago, and I wanted to get up and dance – but I didn't want the audience to see me looking such a fright, so I stayed rooted in my seat.

'I can't believe we're in the royal box as guests of Belinda Carlisle,' Kira whispered in the interval.

'At least we didn't burn her flat down,' I said, shuddering at the prospect.

Belinda invited us backstage afterwards and we went to say hi.

'You were amazing,' I said, hoping we didn't smell too badly of sage as she kissed me on the cheek. We chatted for a while, and I warned Belinda her apartment smelled like a cross between a herb garden and a barbecue, but she was just grateful we'd gone round to smudge it.

'The negative feeling was just where so many people had stayed there, and yet it wasn't really anyone's home,' I explained. 'It's nice and cosy now.' Belinda hugged me.

'Thanks,' she said, and rang the next day to say it was more homely in there now. We're still in touch and she always comes to see me whenever she's in town.

I nearly always stay friends with people I read for regularly. It just happens that way, especially if they come to see you often. I think I see so many celebrities because I treat them the same as everyone else, and can see the truth about their lives – their insecurities and what's really going on away from the PR machine and gloss. They learn to trust me because I say things how they are. I call a spade a spade, and don't put on any airs and graces. People like that.

Maybe that's why I got a call one day from a production

company working on an ITV2 show about girl group the Saturdays. They wanted me to give the girls a reading. It sounded fun, so I agreed.

'They'll come to you,' the producer said, and a few weeks later the film crew turned up, ready to record me giving two of the girls, Vanessa White and Rochelle Wiseman, a reading. They were young, good-looking and bubbly, with a lot of positive energy around them.

'We're really excited,' Rochelle, the tall one, said.

'And a bit nervous,' Vanessa added. I did her reading first, and linked into Spirit straightaway.

'You want to meet someone nice,' I said, and told her all about her past as well as her future. The reading was very detailed, and in-depth, even though it was all on camera, and Vanessa got quite emotional at one point, becoming tearful. But there were plenty of highs I could point out to her, so at the end she felt better. 'Oh my God, that was amazing,' was her overall reaction, and now it was Rochelle's turn.

I tuned in with her father as soon as she sat down. They'd had difficulties in the past, but he wanted to say he was sorry. Rochelle was upset but wanted to hear what he had to say.

'You've met your soul mate,' I told her. I didn't know who she was seeing but I could see they were similar deep-down and had lots in common. 'He gives you stability now,' I said, and she smiled. 'But you might have to walk away to come back,' I added.

We got on well, and after the reading I gave her a cuddle, and kissed her and Vanessa goodbye. They were sweet girls and were forever popping in after that. Vanessa came in for a reading not long afterwards and we went for a coffee. The next time the girls arrived together. It was summer and sweltering hot, one of those days in London when there's no air around. My reading booths are cloaked in thick drapes, which are closed for privacy, and I sat fanning myself, but I was about to melt.

'I'm boiling, girls,' I said. 'Do you mind if I take my top off? I can't concentrate in this heat.'

They started laughing and said they didn't mind, so I sat in my camisole top, giving them a reading. We were all girls together so it was no big deal and I'm not shy about my body – not since I've had a boob job.

'You look fine,' Leigh would reassure me, but I didn't believe him. I wouldn't wear dresses because I didn't have any curves, and wouldn't dream of putting on a bikini on holiday.

'I want some breasts,' I moaned, staring at my reflection one day. 'Maybe I should get myself some boobs as a birthday present to myself,' I thought.

A friend had just had hers done on the NHS and they looked amazing. It wasn't just her breasts that were bigger though – her confidence had doubled, too.

'Do it,' Star said, making an appearance. 'It'll make you happy.'

So I went to see my doctor to see if he could help. 'I'm really unhappy with the way I look' I told him, prepared to have to save up for the operation. But he referred me to a psychologist to see if I was suitable for surgery.

'I can cope with having deformed fingers from my arthritis,' I sighed. 'But I can't put up with not feeling like a woman because I don't have a cleavage.'

I was accepted straightaway. Leigh didn't want me to have it done; neither did my rheumatologist.

'It could be dangerous because of your medication,' he said.

I was on a new drug to stop the inflammation in my joints, which meant I was at a much higher risk of infection. But I didn't listen. I was determined to get my breasts made bigger, and took the first date they could offer. Leigh came with me.

'You OK?' he asked as I waited to be taken to theatre. I nodded, desperate for it to be over with. I'd had twenty operations because of my arthritis, more than enough. At least this one was my choice. But just as my surgeon arrived, a sense of dread flooded through me.

'Won't be long now,' he smiled. 'I'm off to theatre to get ready.' I forced a smile.

'You'll have to do them twice, doc,' I blurted out. 'Something's going to go wrong.'

He shook his head, dismissing what I'd said as pre-op nerves, but it wasn't. I knew there was going to be a complication. Maybe I should have backed out then, jumped off the bed and run out of the hospital, but I didn't. What was I supposed to say? 'Sorry, I'm a psychic and I can see a problem with the surgery, so thanks but no thanks.' They'd think I was crazy.

What they didn't know is that I had to have everything done twice. It's my unlucky number, at least where surgery's concerned. Every time I'd needed an operation because of my rheumatoid arthritis, it never worked the first time. I'd had my toes done twice, my elbows done twice – in fact, everything had to be done again. So why would this be any different? But I stayed quiet this time, hoping I was wrong for once.

'See you later,' I whispered to Leigh, when they came to take me to theatre. He kissed me and I squeezed his hand, wondering what I was letting myself in for. 'Too late now,' I thought. I was on my way down the corridor towards the theatre. Once there, my nerves kicked. 'Please let me be OK,' I begged Star as I took a deep breath, and stared into the anaesthetist's eyes. Then everything went black ...

The operation took two hours, and was apparently straight forward. The surgeon placed implants under my breast muscle making me a curvier 34C instead of an A.

'It all went well,' he told me, when I came round, but I winced. It felt like a truck was parked on my chest.

'Ouch, that hurts,' I muttered, surprised. I'd been told the pain would be minimal afterwards, and thought I'd be able to handle it. After all, I was used to pain. I lived with it every day. I'd expected some soreness under each breast where they'd had to cut it to insert the implant, but why did my ribs feel like I'd been kicked by a horse? It hurt even to breathe.

'It'll get better,' I told myself, taking painkillers, but they didn't touch the pain. I was allowed home the next day, and went straight to bed I was in so much agony. Three weeks went by and the pain by then was even worse. Still suffering, I hobbled to the bathroom and, crying with the pain, took off the sports bra I had been wearing and all the bandages that bound up my breasts. I wanted to see what I looked like and work out why it hurt so much. Inspecting the scars under each breast, I soon realized why. Beneath the right breast, I could see a line of yellow. The scar was filled with pus, but it was trapped underneath the skin. It hurt even to touch.

'You've got to go to hospital,' I heard Star say. 'Now.'

I didn't hang around. It was a Sunday, but I was already feeling feverish and a bit sick.

'I don't care how long I have to wait,' I said to Leigh. 'I need to get down there now.'

Leigh helped me into the car and drove me there. I was sobbing by the time we arrived.

'It's my own silly fault,' I wept, but Leigh kissed me.

'It'll be fine,' he told me.

I was seen immediately and admitted back on to the ward. Doctors did blood tests and the next thing my surgeon was walking towards me.

'We've got to operate to take the right implant out,' he said gently. 'There's poison under it and we can't leave it in case it turns to septicaemia.'

I could feel Star with me, making sure I was calm and not overwhelmed with panic. Her presence was soothing.

'I'll be lopsided.'

'We don't have a choice,' the surgeon said.

Of course, I shouldn't have been surprised. I'd known I'd have to have another operation. Why couldn't that dreaded number two leave me alone for once? I couldn't wait for this second operation to be over. As soon as I came round from it, I could see straight away my breasts were uneven. At least it didn't hurt any more. I was being pumped full of antibiotics, and a few days later I looked at my reflection. It was still a shock. My right breast was flat with a livid red scar across it, while the left was a curvy 34C.

'I'm a freak,' I thought, bursting into tears. It looked as though I'd had a mastectomy, but this was all of my own making. I'd have to live like this for at least three months because my body needed to fight the infection and heal properly. I needed to stop the medication before the next implant was put in, so it didn't happen again. I couldn't feel sorry for myself. I looked awful, but at least I knew it would be sorted out in the future. Women with breast cancer weren't so lucky, and it gave me an insight into what they go through with their body image after having a mastectomy.

'Can I have a prosthesis?' I asked the nurses, trying to be positive. If cancer patients can cope, so could I. It was time to stop moping around.

I tucked the false breast into my bra, and checked my reflection. I looked normal – only I knew that one of my implants was missing. I even went swimming wearing it, and apart from worrying that the prosthesis might float out, I didn't feel self-conscious at all.

Every week I had to go back for check-ups with my surgeon and both of us were surprised to see my left implant drop. My remaining breast was so saggy it looked ridiculous.

'We'll take that one out and do both breasts again,' he decided.

Three months after the first operation, I was back under the scalpel. But this time when I woke up I wasn't in any pain at all, only slight discomfort. My breasts looked and felt fantastic, and healed quickly.

And they were worth it. They've given me so much more confidence, but I wouldn't have any more operations through choice. I almost mutilated myself, trying to look better, even though I know I always have to have double the surgery. It just goes to show that even when you know what's going to happen, like I knew that first breast operation would be problematic and I'd need another one, it doesn't necessarily mean you make a different decision. I was so desperate to look and feel better that I tried to ignore my psychic knowledge, but you can't trick fate. What's meant for you won't go by you. I've tried to change my own destiny a couple of times, and I've maybe managed to delay the outcome, but never change it. So now I listen to my inner voice more carefully because it's always right!

8

A date with death ...

'Shall we go?' Leigh asked, and I nodded. I'd slicked on my favourite brown lipstick and was finally ready. I'd made sure I looked nice, but hadn't dressed up for a nice meal or a trip to the theatre. I was working, but this was just an ordinary reading for Leigh's friends who'd booked me for a party at a house in Enfield, north London.

Leigh had offered to give me a lift because he knew the couple giving the party. At least he knew one of them, Dave King, because they went to the same gym and would chat. They were both into body building, and went training most days. All the lads knew each other, but Dave hadn't booked me because I was Leigh's girlfriend. Becky, Dave's partner, had come in to see me a few times for a reading and had decided to treat him. I was looking forward to it. Party bookings were usually fun.

The house was set off a driveway behind electric gates. 'Nice,' I thought, knocking on the front door. Becky was excited to see me and kissed me on both cheeks.

'Come in,' she said, and led us through to one of the reception rooms.

The house was beautiful – understated, and very modern, but I could tell everything was expensive. All the soft furnishings were muted shades of cream and beige set off by brilliant white. It was crisp, minimal and very chic. Even nicer was the friendly atmosphere. Even though it looked like something out of a magazine, the house wasn't cold, but warm and welcoming. Half a dozen people were there, chatting over drinks. Leigh joined them.

'Can I get you anything?' Becky asked and I shook my head. I didn't drink much anyway, but never when I was working. I needed a clear head to keep up with all the messages for the guests.

'I thought you could do the readings in here,' Becky said, showing me through to another reception room across the hall. I've done corporate parties for hundreds of people where I just mingle, dishing out messages to strangers as they pop up. But at a party booking like this, I always did individual readings, one on one, away from the others.

So I made myself comfortable, and waited. Dave sauntered in, wearing three-quarter length jogging bottoms that stopped above the biggest calf muscles I'd ever seen. They were like massive boulders bulging out from the backs of his legs. Everything about him seemed larger than life – his smile, his personality, his sheer presence, but he wasn't scary. He had a warm, gentle energy about him.

I asked him to shuffle the Tarot cards, and as I began talking I felt the need to lean in and whisper. My voice was so low Dave had trouble hearing what I was saying, but I couldn't raise my voice.

'Someone's listening to us,' I said. 'I don't know if it's the police or someone else, but your house is bugged.' I was convinced there were microphones planted everywhere, and the phones were tapped. 'They're listening to us now,' I told him. 'They're outside, over the road. You're being watched.'

The atmosphere was oppressive suddenly, as if the walls were closing in.

'Watch your back,' I said. 'Not everyone you think is a friend has your best interests at heart.' His head jerked up. 'You're going to be betrayed,' I continued.

The message was coming through so strongly I couldn't hold back. One name kept going through my mind over and over. I repeated it to Dave, and he nodded, his mouth set in a straight line. There was so much to tell him, most of it warnings. The only bit of comfort I could see was that religion was very important to him and he'd converted to Islam.

'Keep an eye on your finances,' I told him. 'I feel a lot of your stuff is going to be taken.'

The messages came in a rush, but they were all warning him to be careful. At the end of the reading, Dave nodded and shook his head. He didn't comment on what I'd said, and I stayed in the room to do the next reading. On the way home, Leigh told me Dave had called one of his friends outside saying, 'We need to talk. There's a problem with one of the guys.'

The rest of the evening had passed without incident, and I forgot about it. A couple of days later, Leigh came home and said that Dave wasn't being as chatty as usual with him.

'What did you say to him?' he asked, but a reading is confidential, just like when a doctor sees a patient. It's the same between psychics and their clients.

'I can't tell you,' I said. 'You know that.'

Leigh understood, but he wanted to sort it out. They weren't close friends, but it bothered Leigh that Dave wasn't talking to him.

'Have it out with him,' I said. 'Better to get whatever's up out in the open.' Leigh nodded.

'You're right,' he said. 'I'll ask him next time I see him.'

So he did, and was surprised when Dave said that the reading was so accurate it had freaked him out.

'It was like she was watching me,' he told Leigh. 'I don't know how someone I'd never met before knew so much about me and my life. I was just spooked, but I'm over it now.'

To prove it, he booked me for another party a month later. Like the first time, Dave went first. I smiled as he started shuffling the cards, but then the most awful feeling of dread exploded through me. My mouth opened and the words tumbled out before I could stop them.

'You'll be dead in two weeks if you're not careful,' I said. 'Please wear a bulletproof vest.'

I froze as soon as I'd spoken. Dave's eyes widened and we stared at each other.

'Oh my God, I can't believe I've just said that.' My hand flew to my mouth and I shivered, but Dave didn't say anything, so I carried on with the reading. Only one message kept coming through: be careful. I couldn't get away from it, and tried to convey the urgency to Dave, but I didn't know what he thought because he didn't say anything.

After he left, Becky came through and I tried to act normally, but I was shocked. I'm a psychic, but it's not my job to tell someone they're going to die, and, to be honest, that was the first time it had ever happened. I didn't see anything, there were no visions or details. It was just an overwhelming feeling that made my entire body come out in goosebumps.

Subdued, I finished the readings, then scuttled into the kitchen where Leigh was having a cup of tea with the others.

'Come on, let's go,' I said. 'I'm tired.'

Leigh drove as I explained. Normally, I wouldn't have said anything to him, but I couldn't keep this quiet. I was sure Dave would tell Becky, and I could trust Leigh.

'Me and my big mouth,' I said. 'Why couldn't I have kept it shut for once?' It was a lesson for me that I needed to try to focus more. It had never happened before but I had to be on my guard now in case I could sense someone's death again.

I wanted to forget about it, but one morning, a fortnight later, I was listening to the radio at work when a breaking news story interrupted the music.

'A man has been shot dead outside the Physical Limit gym in Hoddesdon in Hertfordshire,' the newscaster announced. I froze. That was the gym Leigh went to. My fingers punched in his number on my mobile. He picked up on the first ring.

'Dave King's dead, isn't he?' I said.

I knew before he answered. It was exactly two weeks since I'd predicted what would happen.

'He's been shot,' Leigh said. 'I can't get to him.'

I closed my eyes, trying to block out the picture. Dave had

been peppered with bullets from an AK-47 assault rifle as he came out of the gym. It was a drive-by shooting, and another man, Ian, had survived even though he'd been shot, too. Leigh had meant to be there, but for once had been running late after getting his hair cut. He was now stuck at the end of the road, which had been cordoned off by police.

'It could have been me,' he said, his voice catching. I closed my eyes, grateful for that hair cut.

'I have to ring Becky,' I said.

I'd predicted this, and I felt guilty in some way, as if I should have been able to stop it. But I'd given Dave the warning. What else could I have done?

Becky was a mess and asked me to go over. Leigh drove and we listened to news updates on the car radio. Becky looked tired, and was crying when we arrived.

'I'm so sorry,' I said, hugging her. Her body was shaking, and she seemed so small and fragile.

'Come in,' she said, wiping her eyes.

As soon as I walked into the house, I could sense Dave around us.

'He died instantly,' I told her. 'He didn't suffer. It was so quick.' He wasn't wearing his bulletproof vest, but I didn't think it would have prevented his death. There was too much gunfire and the weapon used too powerful. 'The vest wouldn't have made any difference,' I told Becky.

A friend of Dave's, who had been with him when he was shot, was at the house, too. He'd curled up in a ball in the front seat well of the car. A bullet had gone in his side, but he'd been patched up at the hospital, and was sitting sipping tea. His face was white and he was in shock.

'It wasn't your time,' I told him. 'You weren't supposed to go.'

It was awful, hearing everything that had happened and listening to Becky and her and Dave's little boy sobbing.

'Dave's here,' I kept saying. 'He's OK and just keeps saying how much he loves you.'

He wanted a Muslim funeral, so they had to arrange for a burial as soon as possible after the police released his body. Leigh and I went, and it was a blur of black and emotions. We all met at the house and went straight to the cemetery where Dave was buried. It was a crisp, blowy day and the wind caught all the women's headscarves, making them flap in a funeral salute. Hundreds of friends and family were there, and everyone went back to the house afterwards, but it was quiet and sombre, not like some of the rowdy wakes I'd been to before. Everyone was in shock. Dave was so young, and he had a family. No one could believe that he was gone.

Two guys were jailed for Dave's murder, but I didn't follow the trial or the coverage in the newspapers. I wanted to forget what had happened, not keep going over it. I had the image of his death scorched in my mind, and I wanted to erase it. It wasn't that easy, though. I'd have flashbacks to that moment when I'd told Dave he had two weeks left. He had just stared at me, but it hadn't changed anything. The outcome was the same. Would it have been better not to know?

'I hope I never predict anyone's death again,' I thought, shuddering.

Over the next months and years the dread of seeing such a thing again began to fade. And then one day a young American man came in. His wife had booked him a reading for his birthday, but I could tell he was sceptical.

'Your mother's here,' I told him, linking into Kevin's mum. 'She's sorry she had to leave you.' He nodded, showing no hint of emotion.

'You're from New York she's telling me,' and Kevin nodded again. 'You work in finance and that's why you're here.' He acknowledged it, apparently unimpressed. He was the sort of guy who would never have booked a reading for himself. He didn't particularly believe in clairvoyance, but hadn't wanted to disappoint his wife.

'Your mum's telling me you need to take your dad to a doctor or a hospital,' I said, passing on her message word for word. 'She says its urgent and you should go straight back home to take him.'

Kevin didn't look convinced but his mum wasn't going to give up.

'He has a problem with an artery and his heart will fail if you don't do something quick,' I continued, trying to convey her sense of urgency and desperation. 'She's saying, please son. Do it for me, as well as your dad.'

His face softened and he agreed to go.

'I don't know what I'm going to say to work,' he grumbled. 'I can't tell them the truth – my dead mother's told me to go back to New York to save my dad's life even though he isn't ill – can I?'

'I know it sounds mad but she was adamant,' I said. 'That's all she kept saying. I'm only the messenger.'

I watched as he left, convinced he'd dismiss what I'd said, and let common sense take over. Most people weren't like me. They didn't believe in spirits at all, let alone that they could give us urgent messages. All I could do was try to help by passing those messages on. I couldn't make people listen.

A few weeks later, I walked into work to find a massive bunch of flowers with a pair of legs protruding from beneath them. The flowers moved and Kevin was standing there, smiling.

'I came to say thank you, and sorry,' he said. 'You were right. My dad had a clogged artery, which was about to explode. If I hadn't gone back home and insisted that he have a scan at the hospital, the doctors said he would have been dead within a month.'

I grinned, relieved.

'You saved his life,' Kevin said, handing me the bouquet. I shook my head.

'No, I didn't,' I said. 'You and your mum did.'

All day after he left I couldn't stop smiling. It was nice to be part of something that made such a difference. A man was still alive and a son still had his father because of his mother's love. She'd showed it through me, and it made me feel special. Wanting to help others was one of the reasons I'd decided to work as a psychic. I realized I had a rare gift, and using it could make a difference to other people's lives, not just in passing on messages from Spirit, but in seeing things others couldn't.

I suppose that's what made me say yes when I was approached

by various TV programmes and magazine and newspaper journalists and editors. It wasn't about ego, or trying to grab five minutes of fame. I just wanted to use the media to connect with as many people as possible, and to share as many messages as I could.

I'd been doing articles and columns for psychic magazines, including *Spirit & Destiny*, *Fate & Fortune* and *Soul & Spirit*. And now I was asked to do an unusual page for a major women's weekly magazine, *Love it!* The editor, Karen Pasquali Jones, was at a Disney party where I was doing readings while Mickey and Minnie Mouse danced on a small ice rink. That was one of the biggest and best corporate parties I'd ever gone to, but it was noisy and the queue to see me went all the way through the building. I relied on Star to help me and she came through, connecting me with guests' loved ones who'd passed and giving me message after message.

I always left my business cards at parties, and the following Monday Karen rang, asking to see me.

'You told my friend her boyfriend was cheating on her,' the blonde editor said, her eyes wide. 'And when she went home and confronted him, he admitted it. How did you know?'

I shrugged, completely oblivious. I didn't remember the people I'd met or what I'd told them, so I certainly didn't remember speaking to her friend or passing that message on. In fact, it was all a bit of a blur. I must have seen dozens in a couple of hours.

'Your dad's here,' I said, feeling his presence in her office. 'He says he wants you to make trifle again.' Karen smiled, but she looked a bit shocked.

'I haven't made one since he died,' she admitted. 'It was his favourite, and we'd have it every Sunday, since I was a kid.'

Her dad was chatty and eager to pass on plenty of messages, and Karen seemed happy to hear from him.

'It's not my usual business meeting,' she said after he'd gone. 'But I'd love you to be a columnist for us.'

Every week I had to travel the country with a reporter and a photographer, giving random readings to strangers I walked up to in shopping malls or in the street. That way there was the surprise element, and readers could see it was all genuine. The reporter then interviewed the person I'd jumped on to see how accurate the reading was.

'We'll call it "Street Psychic",' Karen said.

So off I went with Paul Webb, the photographer, and Tracy Johnson, the reporter. We went everywhere, from Scotland to Cornwall. We even went abroad, to Spain and Tenerife, Turkey and Cyprus, as well as to the sets of TV soaps, including 'Hollyoaks'.

We'd be on the road for a few days each month. Sometimes Leigh came with me, and we'd stay in hotels and see hundreds of people. It was brilliant fun, and a great way of convincing the public that what I do is real.

One day we were in Birmingham, and I stopped to talk to a mum who was with her three grown-up children. I'd decided to do crystal readings that day and had a bag of ten crystals with me. I asked her to pick out three and hand them to me. Paul took pictures while Tracy scribbled notes, but I blocked them both out as I connected with the woman's mother.

'Your mum Joan is standing behind you,' I said. 'She wants you to stop biting your nails.' The woman went white, and as I gave her more messages from her very chatty mum, she burst into tears. Her girls started crying when they received their messages from Gran and by the end of the reading they were all in floods of tears and cuddling each other.

After making sure they were OK, we moved on. By the escalator, I gave a reading to a woman who'd lost her dad. He had plenty to say and the messages were so detailed she started crying. This happened to the next woman, who'd lost her husband, and to the next family as well.

'There must be something in the water today,' I said. It was such an emotional day. Usually, we got a few tears as people were put in touch with their loved ones, but not this many. After a couple of hours, a man in a suit came hurrying towards us.

'What are you doing to make all my customers cry?' he said, looking worried. I blinked, confused, and he explained he was the manager of the shopping mall. We'd asked the mall's head office for permission to work there, but he hadn't been told.

'I'm a clairvoyant, giving people psychic readings,' I explained. I didn't know if he was going to ask us to leave and was worried that we might not have enough material for the magazine article. But he smiled.

'You couldn't do me a reading could you?' he asked.

'OK,' I said, 'but only if you promise not to cry.'

Over the months, I became friends with Paul and Tracy, and with Karen, the editor. She'd take me out for lunch or dinner, and then began inviting me over to her house. We stopped talking about business and became mates, confiding all sorts in each other. One evening, after we'd been working together for a couple of years, she leant across the restaurant table.

'I'm going to try for another baby,' she said in a low voice. 'Do you think it will happen?'

I stared at her and couldn't see any sign of a baby. Usually, you can see a fertility sign around anyone who is about to become pregnant, and sometimes even colours for a boy or a girl. I couldn't see anything.

'Not yet,' I said. Then I stopped. I could see something, but it wasn't what she wanted to hear. 'I think you should get a scan,' I told her gently. 'I can see lots of small round things inside you, on your right side.'

'What do you mean?' she asked, apprehensively.

'I don't know if it's cysts on your ovaries, or what, but I can just see loads and loads of round things, like Maltesers, inside you.'

I didn't know what they were but she needed to find out. Karen took me seriously and booked a private scan for the following week.

'They didn't find anything on my ovaries,' she told me over the phone. But I'd seen them, as clear as anything, on her right-hand side.

'Get a second opinion. There's something there,' I insisted.

She didn't, though, and every time I saw her after that I had to bring it up. There were so many tiny round balls inside her, it was beginning to worry me. And then I met up with Karen and saw something good for once, a pink fertility sign all around her.

'You're pregnant,' I said, and she shook her head.

'But I'm going on holiday next week,' she confided, 'and I'm hoping something will happen.'

She came back from her trip to America with a holiday souvenir – she was expecting. Her pregnancy went well until her fifth month, when she started complaining of agonizing pains down her right-hand side. One night she rang to tell me she'd been admitted to hospital.

'I thought I was in labour I was in so much pain,' she said. 'Luckily, I wasn't, but the doctors don't know what's wrong.'

Karen went for test after test, but no one found anything wrong, and she had her baby, a little girl. I went to visit, and was alarmed to see her right-hand side still filled with these round balls.

'Get it checked out,' I urged her.

A few weeks later, I got a text late at night from Karen's husband: 'Karen's in the high-dependency unit in hospital. She has pancreatitis.' Scared, I rang to find out more.

'She was being sick and collapsed on the floor,' Alexio explained. 'They've got to remove her gall bladder. For a while it was touch and go.'

I could hear the emotion in his voice, and their baby crying. I couldn't even send her flowers because they weren't allowed into the unit. It was a month before she was well enough for visitors. I blinked when I saw Karen. Normally, she was outgoing and chubby, but now she was gaunt and pale with dark circles under her eyes.

'I had hundreds of gallstones in my gall bladder,' she told me. 'One of them, which was tiny – only the size of a grain of sand – got stuck in the duct, causing pancreatitis.' She paused. 'If Alexio hadn't dialled 999, I might have died.'

Apparently, it causes such bad dehydration, it's often fatal. She reached over and grabbed a plastic pot.

'Look,' she said, handing it to me. It was filled with what looked like Maltesers. They were dark brown and round. 'They're my gallstones,' she said. 'That's what you saw inside me.'

I stared at the jar, stunned. I'd spotted them at least two years earlier, before she was even pregnant.

'Well at least you're alive,' I said, handing back the jar. 'But I think seeing those have put me off Maltesers for life.'

9

Wherever I lay my Tarot cards, that's my home

Salt spray splashed my sandy feet, the sun high up in the bluest sky kissed my turned-golden-long-ago face and all I wanted was the grey and rain of home.

I'd come back to Tenerife soon after Mum's death, and had picked up where I'd left off. I went back behind the bar at The Queen Boudicca's, out with my friends and to the beach to warm my arthritic joints, but something had changed. Mum's death had ripped away the happiness of that carefree life. It seemed quite shallow now, and I needed more. I missed my life back home, and Dad. He was struggling as much as I was without Mum. Even though they'd split up, he'd never stopped loving her. He didn't know what to do now she was gone, and so I made up my mind to go home.

'Dad needs me,' I told myself. 'Time to move on.'

It was getting to be a habit that I couldn't settle anywhere, but I liked it like that. As long as I had my medicine, and my Tarot cards, I could go anywhere, and do anything. So I packed my bags, and flew back to Britain. I'd never been so happy to see drizzle. 'Home,' I thought. My divorce from Simon had come through and he'd moved out of our old flat, so I moved back in. I rushed round to Dad's as soon as I'd dumped my bags. He was living in a flat near my sister, Julie, not far away, so I was near my family.

'You all right, Dad?' I asked him. He was pleased to see me, and I'd pop in every day, sometimes twice a day, after that. I'd worried that my joy at being home would fade as fast as my tan, but I loved it. Of course, it was weird being around Dad and my brothers and sisters, and expecting Mum to walk in at any moment. But I didn't think I'd ever get used to her not being around. Now I needed a job.

'Let's get a stall at Camden Market,' Julie suggested one day, and I thought it was a great idea. We could sell New Age products, crystals, Tarot cards and pendulums to use for dowsing and answering questions. I loved to ask a pendulum questions and see it swing one way for yes, and the opposite way for no. We did a good trade.

One day, when I was at the wholesaler's picking up some new crystals, the guy there mentioned he'd been let down by one of his usual suppliers and wondered if I knew of anyone who made candles. Ever the entrepreneur, I answered, 'Yes, me.'

'Brilliant, can you do me an order for next week?' he asked.

I nodded, sure I could bash some out. But I blinked when he told me how many he wanted.

'Three hundred?' I repeated, trying to hide my shock. I couldn't back out now, so promised I'd deliver on time. All the way back in the car I was cursing myself. Why did I always open my mouth before I engaged my brain? 'How hard could it be to do that many?' I thought.

Julie laughed when I told her, but soon stopped when I said I was serious. We rushed out and bought everything we needed – moulds, wicks, candle wax – and by that evening my kitchen was a simmering, bubbling, candle factory. Julie and I soon had a system going: wicks in the centre of the moulds, pour in the candle wax melted in my soup saucepan on the stove, then bang it to get out all the bubbles, and fill it to the top.

'We're doing OK,' I said as Julie and I counted how many we'd made. We had just enough by the deadline, and the wholesaler was so pleased he gave us another order, then another. Soon, we were making our own Zodiac-sign moulds, and began selling them on our market stall. They made us a healthy profit. Julie and I were never going to grow rich on a candle empire, but it gave us enough money to live on each week.

Standing in the rain at the market one day, I decided to start doing readings for a living. I'd always done them as a hobby, but hadn't ever charged money. Now I wanted to do it more or less full-time, but I wasn't sure I was good enough.

'Don't be daft,' Julie said. 'You're brilliant.'

But I wanted to make sure I was as good, technically, as I could be. I had Star and my psychic ability, but was that enough? I didn't want to let anyone down who came to see me. The clients weren't going to be curious just about their future or the afterlife. Often they would want answers to specific problems, and to be put in touch with loved ones who'd passed away. That was a terrific responsibility and I needed to know I could deliver every time.

So I decided to enrol in a Tarot card reading class, and found one starting in Walthamstow in East London. Psychic development was one reason for joining the class; building up my confidence was another. The class was run by Debbie and Rose and lasted two hours every Tuesday. People of all psychic abilities attended – some were complete beginners and others, like me, had been reading Tarot but wanted to learn more.

After running through the basic meanings, Debbie asked us each in turn to read our Tarot cards. I turned each one over and just read intuitively, saying what I felt when I saw each card. It was so interesting I was totally absorbed, and it was only at the end I remembered I was in the class, in front of the circle, and would now be given a critique.

'Don't bother coming back,' Debbie said and I felt winded, as if I'd been kicked in the stomach. Was I really that bad? 'You don't need to be here,' Debbie said gently. 'You are truly gifted.'

My shoulders sagged with relief, but I didn't believe I was that good. So I carried on going to the class. I wanted to learn everything there was to know, and, besides, I really liked the girls who went there. It gave me something to talk to Dad about, too, when I went round to visit. 'It's so interesting,' I'd tell him as he pushed back his glasses from the end of his nose, and slowly he became drawn into it. It was like revising what I'd learnt when I told him all about the Tarot cards and what had been said in class. He took it all in, and began asking pertinent questions. He wanted to know more.

'Do you want me to buy you a pack of cards?' I said one day, and he nodded. Dad had always known it was something I did, and that I was psychic, but we'd never really spoken about it. The Spiritualist Church and my gift was something I'd always shared with Mum. Now it was nice to let Dad in, too. So I bought him the same cards as I had – the Tarot of Spirit.

There are so many different types of cards but the colours are beautiful on these, and they're quite abstract. I could look at them all day. 'They're like my babies,' I used to say. They were so essential to everything I did, and how I communicated with Spirit, that I couldn't imagine going anywhere without them. I loved just to hold and shuffle them, and know they were in my bag or pocket.

Every clairvoyant becomes attached to their cards, so it was horrible when I went to do a reading for a group of bankers one night, and someone stole them. I'd laid them on the table, ready to give a reading, and turned away for a split second to get something out of my bag. When I turned back, they'd vanished. 'Has anyone seen my cards?' I asked, panicking. I searched everywhere, but they'd gone. I had another, old pack, but it wasn't the same and I was gutted. After that I bought five packs of the same type of Tarot cards, so that I would always have some spare. I kept them in different bags, and one in a drawer by my bedside.

Dad loved his pack just as much as I loved mine, and he would sit listening, raking his hands through his dark, wavy hair as I explained what they all meant. He'd always liked crystals, and he had them dotted around his flat, but Tarot was new to him.

'I like dabbling in them,' he'd tell me over a cup of tea and, in his case, a cigarette.

'You should give up smoking,' I'd admonish him. I hated it, and his lungs were bad. He'd retired but he'd spent so many years running his own business as a paint sprayer, breathing in all the chemicals, that he was forever coughing. But he wouldn't listen, and I couldn't nag him that much. I loved him and hated not getting on. So I'd open a window, fan my arms around, tutting, and let him get on with it. Truth was, I could never be mad at Dad. He was so welcoming and funny to talk to, I loved going round to see him.

One day, I told him I was thinking of opening a shop. 'I really want to do it,' I said. Julie and I still had our stall, and were making all-right money selling our candles, but I wanted a place where I could do readings as well. I knew that being a clairvoyant was what I was supposed to do, and I'd been ignoring it for too long – angry at Star, then my illness, and grieving for Mum. I'd been telling myself it wasn't the right time, and making up different excuses about not being good enough. Truth was there would never be the perfect time. I just had to take a deep breath and do it.

'That's a great idea,' Dad said when I told him. 'I'll do anything I can to help.'

Julie was just as excited, so we went looking for premises. I didn't need anything fancy – I couldn't afford much – and as soon as I walked into a small shop for rent in Sun Street, Waltham Abbey, I knew it was the one. It was just 18ft by 20ft, but it had a great energy and feel to it. Luckily, it was cheap – £100 a week – so I took it.

Leigh, Julie and my dad all came round to help me get it ready. Between us, we built a cubicle where I could do readings, and painted the shop in taupes, light mocha and fawn.

'Looks more like a coffee shop,' Dad joked, but I could see he was proud of me when it was finished.

'What shall we call it?' I asked and Leigh came up with the name Inner Spirit.

'I like it,' I said, and got a sign writer to put it on the front. It didn't take long to get the shop up to scratch, and I filled it full of crystals, candles and New Age products. Then I made fliers to let everyone know I was there, and put an advert in the local paper. It was the first time I'd ever charged for a reading but my phone was soon ringing.

'I'm really busy,' I grinned, realizing I had no more appointments left for the first week. Dad and Julie took turns to do the till while I was with clients, and I decided to hold courses at the shop in the evenings. I'd found my confidence going to a psychic circle, so why not give courses in crystals, so others could learn to use them too?

'You should teach Tarot,' Debbie insisted. She had become a friend by now. 'You're one of the most gifted readers I've ever seen.'

So not long after I'd been a pupil, I became the teacher in my own shop. The psychic circle was to be held every Thursday, and when ten women came on the first night, a shiver of excitement ran through me. It seemed so long ago since I'd seen Star in my bedroom, and now she'd brought me all the way here. Just a few miles up the road from the old terraced house where I'd grown up, I was making a living from communicating with Spirit and teaching others. It was a good feeling. I didn't have time to dwell on it, though. The people were looking at me expectantly, waiting to begin.

'Right, I'm Jayne,' I said, smiling at them. 'Let's go round the group and find out your names.'

It wasn't going to be difficult to learn them. The first woman was called Pat, so was the second – and the third.

'Oh gawd,' I said, laughing. 'What's going on?'

They were a great bunch of women and by the end of that first night we'd made up nicknames for all the Pats. First, there was Mystic Meg Pat, because she was the spitting image of the TV clairvoyant. Then there was Fat Pat, because she was cuddly. With her red hair and loud laugh, her character was as big as her body. And last but definitely not least there was Table Pat, which was the most ridiculous name but it stuck. It came about because the moment she'd walked into the shop, she'd fallen in love with a table we had for sale. We'd planned to sell just crystals and New Age things, but one day at the wholesaler's I'd spotted the most lovely Indian tables and just had to have them as well. It would have been easier if Table Pat had bought a crystal, but lucky she didn't go for a pendulum because that would have been a right mouthful!

The Pats were all brilliant, but Fat Pat was a natural clairvoyant. She was 60 and every other word was a swearword, but she was so intuitive she amazed us all with her readings. 'You've got to do this professionally,' I told her. 'You're so good.'

Later, when I started working at psychic fayres across Surrey,

I got her on to the circuit with me to build up her confidence. She was really talented, but she needed to know it, so the more readings she did, the more she'd understand how good she was. Seeing people's reactions when you put them in touch with a lost loved one, or tell them something that only they would know, is the confidence booster every psychic needs. Reactions are always a surprise. Sometimes clients burst into tears, sometimes they can't stop laughing, or jump up and kiss you, but it's rare to get nothing back from a reading.

So getting Fat Pat out on the road with me was a good move, and we had a great time together. She's now a professional reader and has appeared on TV. We're still in touch, and I'm so proud she discovered her talent at my first psychic circle.

The class was such a success that we got too big for the shop. The landlord had another one nearby. The rent was the same but it was twice the size. I took it and ended up with both shops.

I started healing sessions in the back of the new shop – Reiki, crystal healing and spiritual healing – and was booked solid straightaway. I'd spent some time training in Reiki, which uses universal energy for healing, and had been intuned (had symbols written on me) as a Master. Crystal healing involves placing different crystals on the client's body to energize the person's aura, and spiritual healing requires using your hands. I didn't charge anything for helping people who were ill, and felt privileged to work with them.

Dad used to ask me about it, and I'd tell him about the people I saw who had cancer or serious illnesses, and how much better they felt after I, or one of the girls, did healing on them.

I still visited him daily. He was a quiet, gentle man, but he was interested in what went on outside his four walls, and in what I did, and I enjoyed telling him.

'Are you OK, Dad?' I said one day. He was pale and seemed quieter than usual, but he nodded.

'I'm fine, love,' he insisted. But I didn't believe him. He had hypotension – low blood pressure – which meant he'd feel giddy and light-headed. He'd also had problems with his prostate, gout and had sores on his legs. Dad had always been a fit man, so it was a shock to see him deteriorate and have to take tablets.

'They want to do some tests on me,' he announced one day, and I stared at him. His eyes looked small behind his thick-set specs, but he still had all his hair and was handsome with his olive skin and big smile. 'It's nothing major,' he said, but he was admitted to hospital for exploratory tests and it knocked him for six. He'd never had a day off work in his life through illness and it was a shock to his system. We all visited him every day in hospital, but Dad looked drained, and weak. He and I were really close, so I tried to talk to him, but he was emotionally exhausted.

'It'll be OK, Dad,' I kept saying, and he'd give me a weak smile, but he just didn't seem right. Even after he came out of hospital, he seemed lethargic and under the weather. He didn't bounce back as I'd expected him too. 'You OK, Dad?' I'd ask every day and he'd nod, but he wasn't convincing and I was worried.

Three weeks passed and I was driving to the wholesaler's to buy new stock for the shop when I suddenly thought about

Dad. 'He's not right,' my inner voice kept telling me over and over. I rang Leigh.

'I think I'm going to go and see Dad instead of going to the wholesaler's,' I said.

As I turned the car around to head back towards Dad's, I felt Star and Mum all around me. I shivered, but as I got nearer to Dad's house, the connection between Mum and I grew stronger. Deep down, I think I knew what that meant, but she and Star kept me strong. 'Look after Dad,' kept going round in my mind, so I wasn't shocked when I arrived to find him looking dreadful, tiny and shrunken in his chair, but when I looked down at his legs, I flinched. They were swollen to three times the normal size. And it wasn't just his legs that were full of fluid. His lungs were filling up, too. It was like I could see inside him, straight to the problem. In his bedroom, the spots of bright red blood on his sheets were unmistakable. I called Julie, who rushed round.

'He's really ill,' I whispered. We tried talking to him, and asking how he felt, but he insisted he was OK. It was no use asking him; he was never going to tell the truth. Dad wasn't a whinger. He was strong, mentally and physically, and he wasn't about to give in now. But his face was white and pinched. His cheeks were sunken, and there were black circles under his eyes. I could see pain etched into every pore and line.

'I'm calling you an ambulance,' I said. He tried to protest, as I knew he would – Dad didn't believe in being ill – but I couldn't just watch him getting sicker and do nothing. Our sister Lorraine had arrived by now and I saw her shudder at the sight of Dad, but we hesitated to make the call, because we knew it wasn't what he wanted. I closed my eyes and felt Mum and Star nearby. That gave me strength. I knew he'd hate me for it, but I didn't have a choice. I couldn't standby and do nothing.

'I'm just going to ring Leigh,' I lied, stepping into the hall. I couldn't make the call in front of Dad. But outside his front door, in the communal hall, I dialled 999. 'Ambulance please,' I said when the operator answered. I kept my voice low because I didn't want him to hear me. After giving his name and address, I went back into his flat to wait.

'I've called an ambulance,' I whispered to Julie, guilt and fear exploding through me. Dad realized something was up.

'You've got to go to hospital,' I said, my voice shaking. I broke down when the paramedics arrived, and he started crying, too. 'I'm so sorry,' I said as he was stretchered to the ambulance. Then I rang my other brothers and sisters.

Dad was taken to Whipps Cross Hospital in Leytonstone. I rang Leigh on the way and he met me there. I was a wreck, but nothing compared to Dad. He had a drip in his arm, and couldn't speak as his lungs filled up with fluid. The doctors talked about pleurisy while Dad rambled incoherently. His heart wasn't pumping the fluids around his body properly and his lungs needed to be drained.

'Is he going to be OK?' I asked. The doctor looked me square in the eyes but there was an involuntary shake of the head.

'You've got to prepare yourselves for the worst,' he said.

I stumbled towards Leigh, who caught me. The others were just as shocked. The doctors were trying to drain off the fluid, but glancing over at Dad I realized it was futile. He was out of it, in a coma. 'He's ready to go,' I thought, a ragged shard of grief ripping through me.

I'd been on my feet for hours by now, and didn't have my medicine with me. Every joint flared with a raw, throbbing pain, but it was nothing compared to the thought of losing Dad. I was in a hospital, so arranged for a prescription of my tablets to be made up, but I didn't care if every part of me hurt. Dad was dying. I needed to be with him, and to help him. I understood that this was the most important moment of my life. I hadn't been there for Mum but she was here, around me now. She wanted me to help Dad.

'Don't be scared, love,' she told me, and I tried to relax. Guilt throbbed inside. Maybe I shouldn't have called the ambulance. Dad hated hospitals, but what else could I have done? I loved him, and wanted to help him. I thought the doctors could have done something to make him better. Now Mum and Star were telling me the same as the doctors. It was Dad's time to go. And he needed me to make it as easy as possible. This wasn't about me and my fear. This was about showing my love for the man who created me, and making his journey onwards pain free.

'We'll help you,' Mum and Star said, and I steeled myself.

Dad was in bed with the curtains drawn around him. He had an oxygen mask on but was still gasping for breath. A monitor tracked every beat of his heart. I watched the line dip and fall, trying to grasp that my dad was dying, and it didn't feel real. I remembered him younger, running behind me when I learnt to ride a bike, watching me play the recorder at school, and more recently painting my shop. My dad had always been so strong, so full of life. He wasn't this man lying here in this bed, struggling to breathe. Julie and I watched as the doctors moved him into a side ward and pumped him full of morphine to help with the pain.

'It won't be long,' a doctor said gently, and I lay down on the bed beside Dad. I was aching from head to toe, but I wanted to help him with his pain, not think about mine. Dad's eyes were closed, he wasn't really with it. I rubbed his swollen hands.

'Mum's here,' I whispered, anxious to do everything I could to make this as easy and painless as possible for him, but it didn't make my guilt any easier to bear. Dad hated hospitals. He'd have preferred to have been at home. But I'd been trying to save him. I'd rung the ambulance, thinking the medics could help. How was I to know it would all be too late, and in vain?

Mum's energy was overwhelming. I could feel her around me, the air hummed with her personality.

'You're not supposed to be on the bed,' a nurse chastised me, but I ignored her. I was with Dad now, cuddling him. I didn't care about any hospital rules. I wanted to be close to him, to hold him.

'It's OK, Dad,' I whispered as Mum's energy grew stronger. 'You can go now.' I opened my eyes and looked at him. His aura was pale yellow. He was weak and in pain. 'Go now,' I said again, and I saw his energy lift. It was as if he lifted above his own body, a shimmering mist. Squeezing my eyes closed, I started to do Reiki on Dad. Even now, I didn't want him to die. Selfishly, I was trying to cling to him, to hold on to him and keep him with me. It was so hard to let him go. I had my favourite crystals with me, as always – rose, angel's hair, pyrite and rootalated quartz – and I kept moving and placing them around Dad. I wasn't fighting Mum. I just hung on to him for as long as I could. I loved him so much. And then I felt him just stop. There was no last breath, no last exhale. He just stopped. Like a clock that had run out of time.

'I love you,' I whispered. 'He's yours now, Mum.' I didn't move. I just lay there in his arms for what seemed like hours. I knew he was safe. Mum and Star had Dad now, but I wasn't ready to get up just yet. He was still warm, still Dad, and I clung to that, drank in his smell of tobacco and Old Spice. After a few minutes I realized that Mum wasn't around any more. She, Star and Dad had left, and I shivered. My heart hurt as much as my joints.

'He's gone,' I whispered to Julie and we fell apart.

I can't remember who called the boys, but glancing at my watch, I saw it was 7am on 12 February, 1989. Adam's birthday. 'Dad's dead,' we kept saying, to everyone it seemed, trying to believe our own words. His body was there, in the hospital bed, but he was long gone. I couldn't feel him anywhere near, and I wanted to be gone, too.

I kissed him goodbye and went back to his flat. I picked up his Tarot cards, put them in my bag, and then I did what I always do when the going gets tough – got going.

This time, Leigh and I decided on Australia. He wanted to become a scuba-diving instructor and I just wanted to get away. So we buried Dad and applied for our visas. Then we boarded a plane for Australia. 'Barrier Reef here we come,' I said, fastening my seat belt. My heart felt heavy, but I was ready for whatever was going to happen next.

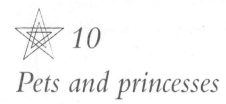

10

Pets and princesses

Through the window of our Blackpool hotel, I watched the rain pouring down. I wasn't looking forward to pounding the streets, trying to persuade people to submit to readings for my *Love it!* magazine column. I loved being a psychic and doing random readings, but I've always hated bad weather, probably because of my rheumatoid arthritis. My joints ache badly enough on most days but they throb with pain when it's cold or wet.

'Don't worry,' the magazine's reporter, Tracy, said. 'That lot look like they'd be interested,' and she headed over to a group of girls, also having breakfast in the hotel. She came back smiling. 'They're all up for a reading.' Paul the photographer was already setting up his camera for an indoor shot. None of us fancied traipsing around in this weather.

Half a dozen girls were sitting at the table, but one in particular jumped out at me.

'Do you mind if I give you a reading?' I asked, and she nodded. Tracy had explained what we were doing but the girl looked sceptical.

'Do you have anything I can hold?' I said. The girl shrugged. 'It's just so I can get a connection,' but she didn't seem to be listening.

Being a psychic, I'm used to cynicism. Many people assume that we're all fakes and rip-off merchants. We're even less popular than traffic wardens and yet we're only here to help. Of course, there's the odd charlatan in every walk of life, but I've never met a rogue clairvoyant yet. Most do what they do because they have a gift and, like me, feel compelled to use it. There are easier ways to make money, and yet most people assume we're on the make or after something, even when, as in this case, I'm offering my services for free.

The girl, who was about 18, had speared her sausage on her fork.

'Let me use that,' I said. She raised her eyebrows, but just by holding on to the fork, I could use psychometry – touching objects to link in to the owner, because possessions hold on to the user's memories.

'Are you happy for me to speak in public?' I said, suddenly very aware of her situation. The girl shrugged again, and so I took a deep breath and began to speak.

'You're seeing two guys,' I said. 'You've got a boyfriend, but you're also meeting up with your ex.' The girl gasped, and I saw Tracy scribbling away while Paul took photos.

'I have a lady here,' I said, seeing the older woman standing next to the girl. 'She says you're going to leave your boyfriend for your ex.' I paused as all her friends looked shocked. 'But she wants to remind you that he's hurt you before,' I said softly, 'and he could do it again.' The same phrase kept coming up over and over. 'The grass isn't always greener,' I said and the cocky girl's face crumpled. I was stunned when she started crying.

'How did you know all that?' she sobbed as her friends tried to comfort her. I didn't answer. I felt bad that she was in such a state. It wouldn't have helped to say, 'well the sausage told me,' would it?

But, to be honest, funny things happen to me all the time. And it's mostly when people don't believe a word I say. One day, a woman came to see me for a reading and as soon as she sat down I could see that her daughter was pregnant.

'You're going to be a gran soon,' I told her, hoping she'd be happy. The woman glared at me.

'I don't think so,' she snapped. 'My daughter's only fifteen.'

I tried to focus to get some other message but that was all that was coming through. It was so strong, even Star couldn't get past it.

'You're wrong,' the woman said after I told her some more details about the pregnancy and her daughter. Ten minutes into the reading she lost her temper and stood up, furious.

'Call yourself a clairvoyant?' she stormed. 'You're talking rubbish and you should be ashamed. It's disgusting.' She was so angry, she threw her chair back and stormed out. I blinked, a bit taken aback. I hadn't had a reaction like that before. The woman hadn't even paid.

'Oh well,' I thought, 'you can't please everyone.' I was only doing my job, but some people don't like hearing the truth. So I tried to forget about it.

'She *is* pregnant,' Star told me to reassure me. And I knew for a fact I was right.

The next morning I arrived for work and found the woman

standing outside.

'I'm so sorry,' she said as soon as I began unlocking the shop. 'My daughter is pregnant, like you said.'

I tried not to smile because she looked genuinely upset and apologetic. She was still talking, saying how she'd gone home in a terrible mood, thinking I was lying.

'I told her what you'd said, thinking she would dismiss it, but she admitted it,' the woman said. Apparently, the girl was four months gone, and had been too scared to tell her mum because she was only young. 'I want to thank you,' the woman said. 'Because of you, we've sorted everything out, and I'm going to help her.' I was glad. Then she held out her hand. Inside was the fee for the reading.

'I walked out yesterday, but I've come back to pay you,' she said. I took the money. I'd earnt it fair and square and it would have been rude to refuse.

'Thank you,' I said, leaning over to kiss her on the cheek. Then I rushed into the shop, grabbed a rose quartz crystal and came running out. 'This is for you,' I said, handing it over. She needed to be calm and positive, and this would help her. 'The boy won't stick around,' I said gently. 'But everything will be OK.'

She nodded and gave me a hug. I never saw her again, but I'm sure she, her daughter and her grandchild are doing fine. I would *know* if she wasn't. She was the first person to storm out on me, but I doubt if she'll be the last. The one thing I tell myself every day is 'never say never'. If you think it won't happen, you can bet it will, so every day I expect the unexpected, and that way I'll never be surprised, or at least, I hope I won't.

One day, a woman came to see me in Selfridges. Tracey was 38 and unusually distant. Sometimes it can be hard to read people if they put up a barrier, but even though Tracey was blasé, I could already see her mum sitting beside her.

'Your mother's here,' I told her, expecting a reaction. Nothing. 'She says she loves and misses you,' I continued. Tracey pulled a face. Her mum gave me her name, the date and how she died along with a very personal message for her daughter. Tracey didn't seem to care.

'Are you all right ?' I asked and Tracey looked at me.

'I didn't come here to listen to my mother,' she said in a very posh voice. 'I just want to know if Bruno is OK.' I frowned, confused.

'Bruno?' I repeated and she nodded. 'Who's that?' I asked and she glared at me.

'My dog,' she said in a harsh tone. Then she picked up a plastic bag she'd placed on the floor by her feet and removed a wooden box. Inside was a clear plastic bag, from which she pulled out a pile of dog's hair.

'This is from my baby,' she said, and I cringed. I didn't know whether to laugh or run away. I love animals but a handful of dog's hair is enough to make anyone feel strange. Gingerly, I put out my hand to take some of the fur. It made me shudder but I held it and asked Star to help me link in to Bruno. Nothing.

'Please,' I willed, bewildered. Star remained quiet.

After a minute, I had to tell Tracey, 'I'm so sorry but I'm not getting anything.' I kept trying, but Bruno wasn't in an obedient mood. After five minutes Tracey snatched back the pile of fur.

'Let's not bother then,' she snapped, putting it back in the bag and wooden box.

'I've got your mum and she's got plenty to say,' I told her but she wasn't interested.

'Awkward,' I thought as Tracey flounced out, but that's people for you. How can she have been more interested in her dog that her own mother? But maybe she had a better relationship with the dog.

Tracey seemed to have started a trend, and I had three other pet owners come in that week, all expecting to talk to their beloved animals. One handed me her dog's collar and Sheba came through immediately. Sheba was a Golden Labrador who'd been put to sleep because she was in enormous pain with her back legs. Her owner was guilt-ridden.

'You made the correct decision,' I told her. 'She wouldn't have been able to walk.'

Sheba didn't blame her owner at all. She loved her. But she wasn't so enamoured with the new puppy she'd bought.

'She doesn't want you to put the puppy in her bed,' I said. The owner nodded.

'The puppy's fine until I put her in the bed to sleep,' she explained. 'And then she yelps.'

The new dog was sensing Sheba, who was jealous. By connecting with her old dog, the owner was able to work out she needed to throw Sheba's bed away and buy a new one for the puppy.

'There you go,' I said, handing back the dog's collar. I was happy I'd been able to help Sheba find peace and the owner accept she'd done the right thing.

It wasn't always that easy to handle the props that clients bought in to help me connect to Spirit. One day, Kim came in desperate to hear from her dad. She was smiley, with curly hair and big, green eyes.

'Bobby's here,' I said as soon as she finished squeezing the life out of me with a bear hug. She gasped while I frowned. 'Kim,' I said carefully. 'He wants to know why you've still got his dirty underwear.' Her hands flew to her mouth. Then she burst into tears.

'I've got it here,' she said, rummaging in a holdall. I stared at her, listening to him complain about her holding on to it. Then it was my turn to gasp. In her hands she was holding his pants, vest and socks.

'Your dad keeps asking why,' I said. Kim was hysterical by now and I felt sorry for her.

'I just can't bear to part with them,' she said. 'They were the last things he wore and they still smell of him.'

Her dad was getting cross but I was full of sympathy. I knew how it felt to lose your dad. I could understand her holding on to the last remnants of him. Bobby was less sympathetic however.

'You can keep the blue jumper,' I repeated, 'but bin the rest.' Kim shook her head.

'I'm never getting rid of it,' she said and I believed her. It's always hard to let go of loved ones, and sometimes their belongings become very precious. It's our last connection with them, and we think that by clinging on to their possessions we'll be able to hang on to them. Sadly, it's not true, but people will keep the most bizarre things. I've been handed someone's mum's ashes in an urn, someone's dad's old dentures, and funeral flowers that had been pressed and I was now expected to read. At least it means I'm ready for anything.

At work one day, my phone rang.

'Is that Jayne Wallace?' a woman asked. Her English was perfect but it wasn't her first language.

'Yes,' I answered, and listened as she asked if I ever did house visits.

'It's for a VIP,' she said. 'Well, in fact it's for a VIP and twenty friends. Tomorrow night.'

'That's a lot of people,' I said. 'I won't be able to do that by myself.'

The woman agreed that I would need to take another clairvoyant with me, and I quoted her a price, which she agreed without hesitation. She said that a car would come to collect me from Selfridges the following night.

'You mustn't tell anyone about this meeting,' she said. 'And I can't tell you who it's for. You won't know until you arrive.'

It wasn't the first time a reading for a client had been surrounded by mystery, so I agreed. Luckily, one of the other girls at Psychic Sisters was free and the next night Jackie and I stood waiting outside Selfridges dressed in our work clothes. Soon, a Mercedes drove up, stopped and a rear door opened. As we sank into soft white leather a woman's voice said, 'You'll have to lose the T-shirts.' She was sitting in the front passenger seat.

'Why?' I said, glancing down at my purple T-shirt with Psychic Sisters written in silver glitter across the front. 'What's wrong with them?'

'We're going to see some Arabian princesses,' she said. 'They're not allowed to consult clairvoyants. So it would be better if you didn't advertise what you do.'

I bit my lip. I'd done readings for Arabian princesses before in Selfridges, and I knew mediums were frowned upon.

'We'll meet them in the stables, so no one sees you,' the woman said. And then, as if to answer the question forming in my mind, she added, 'I'm their bodyguard.'

Jackie and I glanced at each other. Her eyes twinkled with excitement, and even I felt a jolt of anticipation. I hadn't ever been to an Arabian princess's house before, but then I remembered we were sneaking in to see them in the stables, so we were hardly going to be able to see their rich, opulent surroundings.

When we were nearing the secret location, the driver turned down a road, which led on to a quiet lane. Halfway down the lane, the car slowed down next to a café.

'This is us,' the bodyguard said, and we clambered out. She stood beside us and made a call on her mobile as the car drove off. I looked at my watch. It was 7pm.

'I hope this doesn't take too long,' I thought. I was tired and we still had twenty readings to do between us.

Five minutes later, a car pulled up, and the bodyguard nodded for us to get in. As we drove off, she explained that there were two princesses and the rest of their 'sisters' were from orphanages. Their father had chosen to adopt these girls to be with his daughters as they grew up.

'They are schooled at home, and these are the only friends they can have,' the bodyguard explained. 'The king has to be able to trust the friends the princesses mix with.' I nodded as we drove up to some iron gates. 'Say you're hairdressers if anyone asks you,' she instructed, but before I could answer she told us to duck down.

Her face was so serious I slid on to the floor behind the driver's seat. Jackie was beside me with her hand clamped over her mouth. Her shoulders were shaking with laughter and I had the urge to giggle too.

'If the king finds out, I'll get the sack,' the bodyguard hissed and Jackie's shoulders shook even more.

My joints were beginning to ache crouched down out of sight and I hauled myself up as soon as the bodyguard said, 'You can come out now.'

My eyes widened as we passed row upon row of classic cars and Bentleys. Leigh loves cars so I recognized many of them from his magazines and the car shows he'd dragged me along to – Audis, Lamborghinis, and even a Bugatti Veyron, the world's fastest and most expensive road car, with a price tag of £1 million.

'Wow!' I exclaimed, staring at them and imagining what Leigh would think if he was here. We reached a clearing and the car stopped. I stepped out, and stretched, taking in the acres of land.

'Some stables,' Jackie muttered. The block was enormous, and there were tables and chairs outside.

'The princesses will be here soon,' the bodyguard told us. 'Would you like something to eat?' We both shook our heads and stared at two cars heading towards us. A Bentley convertible pulled up, followed by a white Land Rover Sports. Two young girls were driving, and I could see what seemed like dozens of girls in the back. One of the princesses jumped out. She was pretty, and wearing a pink Juicy Couture tracksuit.

'Pleased to meet you,' she smiled, shaking our hands. 'How are you?'

Before I could answer there was a gust of wind, and the sound of a helicopter overhead. I looked up to see one approaching the house.

'Quick, hide,' the princess said, her voice shaking with panic. The bodyguard was already ushering us towards the stable block.

'In here,' she said, herding us into the toilets. 'It's the prince. Don't come out until I say it's safe.' Jackie was giggling again. What would happen if we were found here, wearing our Psychic Sisters T-shirts?

'I'd have asked for more money if I'd known it was going to be like being in a James Bond film,' I muttered. I was tired, and wanted to get on with the readings. I hadn't come here to hide out in the toilets.

'Look,' Jackie said and I stopped scowling. These weren't any ordinary stable toilets. These were royal, with a sofa, and porcelain basins with gold taps, and expensive soaps and hand cream. The actual toilets were in the next room. This was more like a living room – a giant, luxurious living room.

Ten minutes dragged by. Then we heard the whirr of a helicopter taking off again, and five minutes later the door clicked open.

'All set?' the bodyguard asked. At last it was time for us to do the readings.

The princess smiled at me over the table. I could see she was engaged, and the reading was all about her relationship, and upcoming wedding. She seemed happy with what I'd said, and after Jackie and I had given readings for the other princess and the rest of her group, she invited me to see the horses.

'I've got one that's not behaving very well,' she said. 'I'd like you to find out why. Can you work with animals?'

I nodded, taking in the beautiful Thoroughbreds staring at us over the stable doors. The princess told me how much she loved her horses, and how they had their own aeroplane for when they were flown between their homes abroad and London.

'We come here for four months every year,' she said. 'I've got a new horse but I think he's a bit crazy.' We stopped by a brown Spanish horse. 'This is Thunder,' she said. 'He's so moody, and keeps throwing his riders.'

I looked at Thunder, noting his flared nostrils and angry eyes. Very slowly, I held out my hand.

'Easy boy,' I said, stroking his silky coat. He backed away from me. But I didn't give up. I inched closer, and stroked him again. 'He's had a traumatic time,' I said, sensing his fury and frustration. 'He has psychological problems. He doesn't trust anyone.'

I could sense he'd been abused and beaten as a foal. Now he

was nervous around people. He'd throw jockeys and bite.

'He's jealous of the other horses,' I said. 'He was never right. Not since you got him from a horse rescue centre.'

The princess nodded and said that when they brought him home, he was covered in cuts, which took a long time to heal.

'His emotional scars are taking longer,' I said, placing my hands on his flanks. I was a Reiki Master, and could heal people and animals by placing my hands on them in certain positions. 'You need to give him lots of love,' I told the princess. As she watched, I placed my hands all over Thunder to give him Reiki healing. It would take him a while to gain confidence because he had been badly damaged emotionally. Over the next hour, I worked on him, then decided to use crystals and aromatherapy oils to calm him down.

'He'll be better,' I told the princess later. 'But don't expect miracles.'

I didn't charge for healing, but the bodyguard handed me and Jackie an envelope on the way home. I peeked inside mine and saw it was full of notes. We'd been well-rewarded financially for our night's work.

I went back, for free, to work on Thunder. The next time I took a crystal wand to massage him. The wand was made of amethyst, which was round at one end and pointed at the other. Slowly, I worked on all his energy points, watching him stamp his hooves, then gradually become calmer.

'It's OK, boy,' I soothed, running the wand over his silky coat. Over the weeks, he became more placid, and happier.

'He's healed now,' I told the princess, feeling proud of

Thunder's progress. 'Anyone can ride him now.'

She smiled, and asked me to watch her ride him around the sand school so she could test him for herself.

'He's a different horse,' she said, grinning.

She was so excited she asked me to heal four more horses, which I did.

'You've got the most amazing healing hands,' the princess told me. 'I don't know what I'd do without you.'

11

Letting go

Every time I closed my eyes I saw him. His face was out of the water, but his body was half submerged. He was alive but growing weak. My head throbbed, the same as his did. My body ached where he'd battled to reach the shore. My panic rose up, choking me, as panic choked him. I couldn't shut off. When I woke, he was the first thing I thought of. When I tried to rest, his image was there, flashing before my closed eyes. In my dreams, I was tormented trying to reach him but always being thwarted. And now, I grew weaker, just as he did, thousands of miles away.

'This is agony,' I told Leigh, fighting back tears.

I could feel this man's despair at being lost. I could sense his body losing the fight to stay alive. He was barely clinging to life, and I knew where he was when no one else did. Yet it wasn't enough.

'Why won't they fly me out there?' I raged. 'I can find him.'

Twenty-four hours earlier I'd received a text from a friend, asking me to get in touch with a friend of hers. 'She needs to speak to you urgently,' the message had read. 'Somebody close is missing.'

That somebody was a millionaire, who'd vanished after going

out on his luxury yacht. It had somehow crashed into another boat, and exploded. The man hadn't been seen since. I'd rung the woman immediately. I had grown close to our mutual friend over the past few months. Of course, I wanted to help.

I squeezed my eyes shut as the woman told me, 'No one knows where my son is.' As she spoke, I saw that the captain and rest of the crew had escaped unhurt. Then I saw him, lying on rocks, with his lower body still submerged in the sea.

'He's alive,' I told her, 'but he's weak and half in water.'

As I focused I could see a red shirt and gold-rimmed Ray Bans.

'Yes, that was what he was wearing,' his mother confirmed.

I took a deep breath, trying to see where he was. I was on a large set of rocks, but there was nothing to identify them. I was surrounded by sea. Then I shuddered.

'He's slipping away,' I said, hearing his mother gasp. I wish I could have phrased it better, or softened the blow, but the image was so strong I had to describe it exactly as I saw it.

'They're searching in the wrong place,' I said, realizing that the rescue party weren't near him. 'They need to get the helicopters looking in the opposite direction.'

The missing man's mother began to cry, and explained it would be hard to tell her husband and the search and rescue team to look elsewhere based on the word of a clairvoyant. Her family didn't believe in them, and she was scared they'd think she'd gone crazy with worry.

'You have to act fast,' I said. 'He's still alive but you need to find him soon.'

I was surprised to be asked to help, but now I was getting frustrated. The woman had called because our friend had told her about me, but what use was I if the family didn't act on what I saw and said?

It was torture for me to link in to her missing son and to feel his pain, and his hope fading. I could tell he'd felt the connection between us and was so alone he'd been grateful for me being there. But the bond between us was so strong now, I could see, taste, hear and feel everything that he did, and it was awful. He was thirsty, hungry and growing weaker by the hour. He couldn't move. He wasn't even strong enough to crawl out of the sea on to the rocks.

'Please,' I said to his mother during our endless messages and phone calls. 'Get me out there, or at least give me a map.' I knew I could scour the countryside and pinpoint him. But it was no good. She wanted my help, but she also knew no one would listen to her until it was their last hope. Hour after hour dragged past.

'He's dying,' I realized. Desperate, I called his mother. 'You've got to let me do something,' I begged. 'Tell me I can come and I'll jump on the next plane.'

They didn't even need to buy my ticket. I'd have gladly paid for it myself. I couldn't stand back and feel the man's life force ebbing away. I had to help, but I needed their permission.

'I'll see what I can do,' she said, but I knew it wouldn't be enough. By the time she got her husband's permission, her son would be dead. My head throbbed even harder.

'Why can't they listen?' I thought. 'It'll be too late.'

I slumped in the chair in my living room, watching the hours pass. With each one my head hurt more, and my body drained of energy.

'I can feel him dying,' I said to Leigh the next day. 'I can't switch it off.'

Half of me wished I could sever the connection. It was too painful to feel his despair, hear his thoughts, but the other half of me, the stronger side, was relieved to be there. At least, I could send him healing thoughts and energy. I could help him be calmer, make his passing easier. All day I sat, my head in my hands, begging Star to help me. She and I deluged the man with positive thoughts and healing.

'It will be OK,' I told him over and over, while Star radiated calmness.

'Tell Mum I'm safe,' he said, and my shoulders sagged. He'd given up the fight. 'I'm happy,' he said. Then he lapsed into a coma, and a few hours later he was gone. I dropped my head and began to cry.

'It's too late,' I said, watching the messages from his mother ping on my phone. She was desperately trying to persuade her family to listen to me, but it didn't matter now, and that hurt. A man had died whom I was convinced I could find if I'd been given the chance. It wasn't fair.

'I could have saved him,' I said. 'It's such a waste.'

Not long afterwards, the rescue team found the missing millionaire. He was lying on rocks, half in and half out of the sea. I didn't feel any satisfaction in being right, just sadness that I hadn't made a difference.

I don't know why but they sent me a picture of his body being recovered. It wasn't gruesome. It was a snap of what looked like someone sleeping. I took in the red shirt, and jagged landscape, lapped by waves. It was exactly how I'd seen it, but what good had it done, seeing that scene? I'd been able, along with Star, to send him some healing to make his passing a little more bearable, but that was all.

The sadness lingered with me. Then the following year the friend who'd told the millionaire's mother about me came to see me in Selfridges.

'I have someone who wants to meet you,' she said. The tanned man who was with her looked exactly like the millionaire who'd died, but younger.

'Is this ..?' I began, and my friend nodded. This was the millionaire's brother. I was pleased to meet him and led him through to the reading booth. Instantly, I connected with the missing millionaire who told his brother he was safe and not to worry.

'I'm so sorry,' the young man told his brother, very upset. He felt responsible for them not looking in the right place, and for not listening to me, but both of us understood why.

'He doesn't blame you,' I told him, and could see how much better that made him feel.

It was good to link in to the man and feel his energy, and how at peace he was. It had been traumatic being with him as he died, and I was glad he and his brother could be together again, through me.

I'm still sad I couldn't help him, but I have managed to track down other missing or lost people, although the outcome's not always as expected. One day, about ten years ago, I answered the phone to Theo, who was Greek. His English wasn't brilliant, and I had to concentrate to understand what he was saying.

'I want you to find my little boy,' he said. Then he told me how the child had been taken from his garden a decade earlier, when he was just four years old.

'He's my only child,' Theo said. 'I have to see him.' He began to cry, which made it even harder to pick out what he was saying. But I felt Star near me, making it easier. I just had to close my eyes, and relax, knowing that it would all make sense.

Theo's story was tragic. After his little boy was snatched, his wife went to pieces. She'd let the child play outside in the sun while she washed up, and when she'd gone to check on him, he'd vanished. They'd called the police, and hunted everywhere for him, but hadn't found him, or any clue to where he was. She blamed herself for leaving him alone, and eventually killed herself. Poor Theo had promised himself that he would find their little boy, and would never give up. Now he'd come to me for help.

'I heard you are good,' he said, his voice cracking.

Theo came from a village just outside Athens, and I could tell already that his son had been taken by travellers.

'He's not dead,' I told Theo. 'The woman who took him did it on the spur of the moment. She'd recently lost a child and decided to take yours when she saw him.'

Of course, it was wrong. A family had been destroyed, a mother had killed herself, overwhelmed by the guilt. But the woman who'd done this loved Theo's son. I could see that she took good care of him and he was happy.

'He's with a travelling circus,' I said, even though it sounded odd. I could see a trapeze, clowns and a marquee. The circus went all round the Greek islands, the mainland, Portugal and Spain. 'They left on a boat as soon as they took him,' I said.

The police search had drawn a blank. Theo said there had been sightings of his son in different countries. He'd never given up, and constantly put up posters of him, asking if anyone had seen him. But as more years passed, it became more difficult. The pictures he had were of his son as a young boy. Ten years had passed. He would have changed, and no one knew what he was like now. His blonde hair may have darkened, he could have got fatter, or more tanned. It was like looking for the proverbial needle in a haystack.

But I was sure if Theo sent me maps and a photo, I would be able to link in to the boy's whereabouts. I stared at the unfamiliar names of towns and villages, and felt Star's prescence. When my eyes flitted across a certain place, I'd feel that he'd been there. Then I'd email or text Theo, and he'd go and look.

I was amazed by his love, and how it hadn't faded over time. He still loved his son, and was as determined to find him as he had been at the awful moment when the child went missing. But whenever he turned up at the places I mentioned, he'd just missed his boy.

'Yes he was here,' locals would say when he described his son and said he was part of a circus. I worked out I was about two weeks out of sync, but I didn't know how to catch up. I wasn't able to predict where he was going. I could only link in to say where he'd been. I told Theo to look for posters and signs of where the circus was going next, but he said there weren't any. Maybe, as the months passed, the couple who'd taken the boy, realized Theo was tracking them, so deliberately kept their next destination a secret.

This went on for years. Theo would call every couple of weeks. I would tell him the latest place he'd been, and he'd go there and get confirmation. It wasn't helping him to find his son, but it must have made him feel closer to him, knowing he was walking the same paths, and looking at the same buildings as his only boy had done just a few weeks earlier. Whenever I had a spare moment, I'd stare at the maps, let my fingers caress that old, precious photo. And I'd always ask the same thing – 'Where are you?'

Then one day I felt an overwhelming certainty that he was in Portugal. I could see him, a teenager, almost a man, working behind a stall at the circus. He was handing out prizes and smiling. I even got the town's name, and, with excitement jangling in my stomach, I rang Theo.

'You've got to go there,' I said, spelling out the unfamiliar town. 'He's there. You'll find him. I know it.' Then I paused. 'I don't think you'll get the outcome you want,' I said gently. I couldn't feel a happy ending, but I didn't know why.

'But it's my son?' Theo kept asking.

'I'm sure it is,' I insisted.

Theo had enough faith in me to go straight there. I couldn't relax, knowing he was about to meet his son.

'Sit down,' Leigh said that evening, but I was too jumpy. I couldn't wait for the call to tell me I was wrong, that they would be reunited happily after all. I grabbed the receiver as soon as the phone rang the next day.

'Was he there?' I demanded. Theo was sobbing, but I couldn't tell why.

'Yes,' I eventually made out through the crackly line, and his tears. 'He didn't want to come home. He's happy with them.' I sighed. 'I'm happy he's OK,' Theo kept saying, but he was broken-hearted that he'd lost his son again after finding him.

It was hard to understand, but his son had been so young when he'd been taken that he'd soon got used to the couple being his mum and dad. They hadn't mistreated him. In fact, they'd loved him, as if he was their own. And he'd been part of the circus community. They'd all accepted him and treated him like the couple's son. He had friends and 'family' there.

'He doesn't know me,' Theo said. 'I'm not his father now.'

They stayed in touch, and his son even went to visit Theo, but they'd been apart for too long. They were like polite strangers, not father and son, and no matter how hard they tried they couldn't get back those lost years.

'I'm still happy,' Theo said a few months later. 'I know he's alive. That makes me smile.'

Just then I realized his wife was with me. She wanted to let Theo know how proud she was of him, and she wanted to thank him for finding their son.

'She loves you so much,' I told him. 'You did the best thing.'

I'm still in touch with Theo, and he and his son still see each other. One of them will fly to see the other every few months. They're friends, and Theo is grateful to have his son in his life.

'He's my flesh and blood,' he said. 'I couldn't give up on him.'

It's not just parents who feel like that. One day a woman rushed in to see me, her face swollen and her eyes red from crying.

'I've come down from Norfolk to see you,' she said, thrusting a photograph at me. 'You've got to help me find her.'

I glanced down at the picture. A tabby kitten stared into the camera. She was only two months old and had gone missing a few weeks earlier.

'Please tell me she's OK,' she said. 'I'd hate to think anything bad had happened to Honey.'

Holding the photograph between my fingers, a number flashed in my mind.

'Do you live at number fifteen?' I asked her and the woman shook her head.

I focused, trying to see where the kitten was.

'She's three streets away from you in a house with the number fifteen on the door,' I said. 'A woman has her.' That was all I could get, but it was enough. A couple of days later, the woman rang to say she'd found Honey.

'I scoured all the streets around mine, and knocked on every door with a fifteen on it,' she said. 'I felt a right idiot asking, "Have you found a tabby kitten?" I was about to give up when a woman said she had.'

She'd found Honey lost in the street behind her back garden, and had taken her in. She hadn't known how to get in touch with the owner as the kitten wasn't wearing a collar. So she had started looking after the tabby, hoping someone would be in touch.

Of course, she had grown close to Honey, but because she loved her she knew she had to let her go. That's how Theo felt, and letting go of his son was his way of showing just how deep his love went. It was the most selfless act I'd ever witnessed, but I think if you try to keep someone, or a kitten, who doesn't really want to be there, it's suffocating. Honey and George's son would have resented being trapped. All of us are free, and should be able to choose how and with whom we live our lives. It's the ultimate sacrifice you can make, putting another's wishes before your own.

 *12*

The dead can't hurt you –
only the living can!

The look of my left foot made me shudder. Every swollen, deformed joint had been removed, each toe pinned with metal, and now it was encased in a specially made plaster-cast boot.

'No walking on it for eight weeks,' the surgeon insisted and I spied the crutches beside my bed. I was in hospital after having yet another operation to take away pieces of my body that were slowly being ravaged and destroyed by rheumatoid arthritis.

'I need a holiday,' I sighed to Leigh. But where could I go, hopping along on one foot?

'Let's get you home,' he said, handing me the crutches.

I gingerly tucked one under each arm and tried to walk.

'Easy,' I said, ignoring the pain that was gnawing through my elbows and in my left toes. I'd needed the surgery after the 'knuckle' on every one had become so badly affected by the rheumatoid arthritis they'd all popped out of the joints, leaving me hobbling and in agony. Now, at least, I was recovering.

'One small step for Jayne Wallace. One giant leap for psychics,' I joked. I was getting the hang of the crutches now. Leigh rolled his eyes, grabbed my bag and helped me out to the car.

Back home, I watched TV, read magazines and was soon bored. 'Better do some admin,' I thought, putting on my laptop. Just then my email pinged and I read a message from a lady at Warner Leisure holidays.

'We'd love to meet you about working together,' her email read. I answered straightaway, explaining that I couldn't meet anyone because I couldn't walk.

'Well, shall we come to you?' the woman, called Jane, replied.

So a few days later she and her colleague Lyn were sat in my living room, asking if I'd host a few 'Haunted' weekends at some of their hotels.

'Lots of the guests report seeing ghosts,' Jane said. 'And we'd love to organize a ghost hunt.' I nodded, and had an idea to go one step further.

'Why not go the whole hog and have psychic development weekends?' I suggested. 'I could teach them how to read Tarot, and tap into any psychic abilities they have, during the day and go on ghost hunts in the evenings.'

Jane loved the idea and I agreed to host a 'Haunted' weekend over Hallowe'en. That would give my foot enough time to heal, and for them to advertise the ghost hunt. I was excited because it was something new. Of course, I'd grown up seeing ghosts, so to me that side of it was normal.

'The dead can't hurt you – only the living can,' Mum had said when I first told her about the spirits I saw in my bedroom at night. I couldn't remember a time when I hadn't seen ghosts. First, they'd appear in the gloom, but as I grew I'd glimpse them in daylight. They knew I wasn't afraid of them and so they didn't need to hide in the shadows. They were as real as the living. But although they didn't scare me, I knew to treat them with respect. If a person was evil while they were alive, they probably weren't going to have changed in Spirit. So I never took chances. A bad 'un is always a bad 'un, dead or alive. And, luckily, I could tell from the energy in a room what kind of ghost we were going to encounter.

So as soon as I arrived at Littlecote House Hotel, in Hungerford, I knew our guests wouldn't be disappointed. Littlecote is the most breathtaking sixteenth-century mansion. Henry VIII was introduced to his third wife-to-be, Jane Seymour, here in 1520, and the place looked like it had hardly changed in all that time. It has low beams, a medieval banqueting hall, its own chapel, beautiful grounds – and a lot of ghosts, including one very nasty spirit indeed.

I was shown to the Queen Elizabeth Suite, which had a bathroom bigger than my house, thick curtains around an ornate four-poster bed, and a haunted room next door.

'This is beautiful,' I said, putting my bag down and taking in the rich, opulent surroundings. The windows were floor to ceiling, looking over the most stunning grounds. My bathroom had an iron-claw bath in the middle, and a walk-in massage shower, and yet I couldn't relax. I could feel the most oppressive atmosphere, as if something nasty was seeping through the wall connecting it to the haunted room next door. The atmosphere was so heavy I literally felt sick to my stomach and I wondered if I was going to be able to sleep. This was an intense spiritual energy, which would not be ignored.

'I'll be fine,' I thought, making sure I imagined a circle of bright white light around myself. Over the years, I'd taught myself to be careful. I would open myself up to Spirit by focusing on my chakras. These are seven 'wheels' in the body, which refer to the swirling life-force energy coming from six actual points running along all of us, from the base of our spine to the middle of our forehead. The seventh chakra is higher than we are, and it's this that connects us to Spirit. But every night I would close myself down for protection. It can be draining to see, sense and hear spirits and we all need to rest. So I can open and close myself at will, using my chakras like a key opening a door.

After meeting our ghost-hunt guests, another of the Psychic Sisters, Lindy, and I sat the group in a circle and taught them to open and close themselves down. We needed to make sure they were protected. Seeing a ghost for the very first time could be scary for some people – especially the sceptics, who'd only come along to scoff at us. When the non-believers came face to face with a spirit, they usually became hysterical. And you never knew what kind of spirit we were going to encounter, but if it was anything like the bad, heavy vibe up in my room, it wasn't going to be pleasant. Just walking from my room down to the banqueting hall where we all had dinner I'd come across an energy that had made me gasp, it was so strong.

'Are you the same spirit from upstairs?' I asked, but there was no reply.

I remembered its strength now as I told the group to imagine opening up each chakra as if it was a flower, one petal at a time. Once I was sure they could close them down as easily, we were ready to go.

'We just have to join in a circle so we can put ourselves in a protective bubble,' I told them, asking them to visualize the white light I was projecting around us.

Some of the group of around thirty began to giggle with nerves, but they soon stopped when the chandelier above us started swinging and we could hear bangs and crashes from around the house.

'The spirits know we're coming,' I said. 'And some of them aren't happy about it.'

I didn't want the group to be completely freaked out, so decided to take them outside into the garden. Earlier I'd spotted a spirit out there, next to a ramshackle little house. I'd only glimpsed her very quickly, but could tell straightaway she was friendly. I usually attract the attention of spirits who need help, or who are stuck on this plane, and can't move on for some reason. This woman gave me the feeling that she needed something. So I led the group along the path to the old house. As soon as we arrived, the words 'witch's house' popped into my head.

'Who can smell anything?' I asked quietly. The overwhelming scents of lavender and rosemary filled my nostrils. Others could smell it, too. I stepped inside, into what would have been the kitchen. It was falling down, but there was more to it than that. With every step, the house seemed to buckle and sway, as if it was angry we'd dared to enter.

'I want to go upstairs,' I said. Something up there was enticing me, but the old staircase was so steep, it would be like crawling up a ladder.

'Let's go one at a time,' I whispered, beginning the climb. The smell of lavender became stronger. My body was tingling now and I realized the spirit I'd seen earlier was a powerful white witch. She used her powers only for good and she had a pure, beautiful energy. I could feel her deep in my stomach, as if we were connected. Lindy felt the pull, too.

At the top of the stairs we stood in a huddle, and I said a prayer to bring her energy close to the group. We were soon all swaying, the pull of the white witch was so strong. Daniel, one of the men on the course, who had been sent on the weekend by his wife, had amazing natural psychic ability. Previously, he'd had no idea of his powers and had been so shocked to discover them that he'd spent most of his time so far in tears. Now he stepped forward to the front of the group.

'We're here,' he said gently. 'We can help you.'

As he spoke the white witch appeared before us, the scent of lavender, herbs and rosemary so strong I was sure I'd never get the smell off my clothes. Her straight brown hair hung down to her slender waist. She was wearing a long white dress, and was so naturally pretty, she looked just like an angel.

Lindy stepped forward to stand next to Daniel, and I could see her connect strongly. The white witch was coming through her.

'I'm the protector of the house,' Lindy said, her voice higher than usual. 'I look after all the lost ones.'

She had a maternal energy, although I could tell she wasn't a mother. Just then I spotted a young, black boy behind her, hiding in her skirts. He was about seven or eight, but very small – tiny for his age. He'd been brought to the house from Africa as a slave. He died in the house, and now clung to the white witch, who looked after him and the other children.

I shuddered, aware of another energy outside the house. It was cold, hard and I could tell this man had mentally and physically abused the children here. But he couldn't get near to the little boy now. The white witch wouldn't let the man inside the house. She had promised to keep the boy and the others safe, and this was their haven.

'Thank you for looking after them,' I thought, hoping she would hear. She had filled the house with love for all these lost child spirits, and had become their spiritual mother. It was lovely to know that kindness like that didn't die with the physical body. Spirits could still perform great acts of generosity, even when they'd crossed over, and that put me in awe of the white witch.

'Let's go back to the main house and leave them in peace,' I told the group.

No one spoke as we made our way out of the house and over to the chapel in the hotel. The energy inside was amazing, and I was drawn to a wooden box, which contained children's clothes. I stumbled over the word 'children', though. The clothes were actually those of a baby who had been burned alive in the fire in the haunted bedroom. I shivered – the same dark energy loomed over me that I'd felt briefly in the witch's house and upstairs in the bedroom. Some of the women in the group were scared and clung together.

'No one has to come who doesn't want to,' I told them. 'But you'll be safe with Lindy and me.'

We were going up to the haunted bedroom. Everyone went silent but no one backed out. As we neared the room, the corridor, which just a few moments before had been cosy, became so cold we could see our breath, coming out in big, white puffs. Outside the room, I threw the protective bubble around us once again. Then I took a deep breath and opened the door.

It was gloomy inside, and even colder. A wooden four-poster with red curtains around it dominated the room. Along one wall was a giant beige stone fireplace. A musty odour made my nostrils twitch and eyes smart. One of the women on the course, Alice, volunteered to lay on the bed, and we all placed our hands on her to give her our energy so we could connect with the spirit.

Immediately, she started twitching, and then she opened her mouth wide and started screaming. It was the sound of pure terror escaping from deep inside her. She was thrashing around now and began to screech, 'Get him off me.'

I couldn't see the dark energy but I could feel it and just as I went to move forwards, it grabbed Alice by the feet and pulled her. We all saw her move and she began to scream again. As her voice filled the room, the rest of the group all heard the same voice inside our heads. It was a deep male voice telling us, 'Get out of my room.'

I wasn't scared but some of the others were. Two of the women wanted to run, but we had to help Alice.

'The dead can't hurt you,' I told them. 'He won't harm you. You're safe.'

He was such a strong, bad energy, though, that I didn't want to antagonize him. Alice was sobbing. She could see everything that had happened in the room. He'd 'shadowed' her – entered her body, like Sam (Patrick Swayze) did with Oda Mae (Whoopi Goldberg) in the film 'Ghost'. So Alice could see the man taking the baby from its mother, a young maid. He was furious that she'd had the baby, which was his, and he grabbed the newborn and threw it on the fire, watching it burn alive. Then he murdered the maid.

Quickly, I placed one hand on Alice's head and the other over her heart to take the negative spirit out of her. She instantly came out of the trance and, relieved, I could see that she was back to being herself again.

'That was the strangest experience of my life,' she gasped, shocked. 'I saw everything.' I hugged her. It must have been awful to witness such an atrocity.

'Let's do a blessing spell,' I said, 'so we can cleanse the room of this energy.' I asked the group to form a circle and hold hands. 'Close your eyes,' I whispered. Then, in an atmosphere of anticipation and fear, I called upon our spirit guides, guardian angels and spiritual loved ones to come forward and protect us in the room. I had brought a large smoky quartz crystal with me, and now held it while calling upon the elements Fire, Air, Water and Earth to bring power and strength to my cleansing spell – Fire to burn away the negative energy, Water to wash away the bad vibes, Air to blow away all ill feeling and Earth to ground us. I asked the group to repeat the spell after me, three times:

'Protect this space with all your might

Fill the room with love and light

Bless the Spirits that haunt this space

Help them cross over to the light

So Mote it be!'

As they repeated the spell, I lit a black candle and held it to create a circle of white light to give the room some peace. Then I sprinkled sea salt, sage and lavender around the room in a circle to cleanse it, and placed the candle inside it. Closing my eyes, I visualized a black cloak wrapping around me and the group, and imagined a wall of mirrors to reflect all the negative energy away and replace it with love. Instantly, I knew the murderer had gone. A sense of calm filled the room.

'We can go,' I said, but as we left, I noticed a wooden staircase leading, I presumed, to an attic.

'He's up there,' I said.

'We're not allowed up there,' one of the women said instantly, her voice shaking. She was right. The group had seen enough for one night.

'You wait here,' I told them. 'I just want to take a peak.'

I hurried up the stairs into the old attic. Sour saliva flooded my mouth as soon as I stepped inside. I thought I was going to be sick, the air and energy was so foul. 'He's here,' I thought. I could almost taste his hatred, but underneath his foul energy was the mother's. The room was filled with her tears, and her sorrow. It was overwhelming. I'd never felt so much grief.

'I'll deal with this another time,' I thought, rushing back down to the group. I led them quietly back to the chapel, and we stood around the wooden box containing the burnt baby clothes, and said a prayer. I hoped it helped the poor little soul who wasn't given a chance.

That murderer wasn't the only bad spirit I'd ever come across. I once came face to face with one during a reading. I'd agreed to see Julie, a woman in her thirties, at her house in a smart suburb of London. She was quietly spoken and wearing very nice clothes. I thought she might be a lawyer, or some kind of businesswoman, so wasn't expecting the message that came through for her.

'I have a man here called Michael,' I said, shuddering involuntarily as I felt the connection. He was so full of anger he even snarled when telling me his name. She went pale but just stared at me. I closed my eyes and felt a fist slam into me. Of course, he couldn't physically punch me, but Michael really wanted to hurt me, so he was showing me what he'd like to do.

'He hit you,' I said, and her eyes darted to the floor. 'He beat you.'

She didn't speak but when she looked at me next her eyes were full.

'He terrified you when he was alive,' I said quietly, my voice snagging over the words. I could see him kicking and punching her, the bruises he used to leave just a physical mark and nothing compared to the fear she held inside. I could see her being battered unconscious by him and lying in a pool of her own blood. There were two young children – hers – screaming her name and crying next to her, thinking she was dead. The scene switched to outside. Michael was there. I could feel a noose going round my neck and tightening. He'd hung himself outside on a tree.

'He did it to spite you,' I whispered as she began to cry silently.

I realized the whole story now. She'd been pregnant with his baby and he was so angry, he'd punched and kicked her in the stomach until she lost it. Then he'd killed himself.

'He's proud of everything he did,' I said, shocked. 'He's pure evil.'

She nodded as I pulled my energy away from his. I couldn't stand to have him near me and closed myself down. I wanted to have a shower and scrub myself clean, so I did the spiritual equivalent. I did a cleansing spell to get rid of every last trace of him around us, and in Julie's house. I didn't want him staining one bit of air that any of us breathed. He'd done enough damage while he was alive. I wasn't going to let him traumatise her, or their children, any more now that he was dead.

Sobbing, she told me he'd been her husband and had treated her and their children so badly they'd been left mentally as well as physically scarred. I sat talking to her all afternoon, and did healing on her. I also asked Star to send some psychic healing for Michael as a way of him finding a way to move on. He needed to atone for what he'd done, and to learn from his hideous mistakes. She told me that he eventually apologized for what he'd done. It didn't help Julie but it made me feel better.

I always seem to attract the most traumatised, needy spirits, who have lost their way. Friends tell me I'm kind and go out of my way to help people here, and I'm humbled by that. I just try to treat people how I would like to be treated, and that goes for the living and spirits.

On our next ghost hunt was at Thoresby Hall Hotel, in Nottingham, on the edge of Sherwood Forest – Robin Hood country. On that occasion, we were able to help a spirit trying to find her lost child. We'd waited until it had grown dark to go outside, and as soon as the group began to walk along an overgrown pathway, we could all see a white glow in the distance. As we neared it, I could see a lady blocking the pathway, wearing a long, blue, lacy dress. Her eyes were as brown as her hair, and they were staring straight at me. When I peered closer, I could see her feet were off the ground and that she was hanging from a branch. There was a noose around her neck, and her head lolled to one side. But she hadn't killed herself. She'd been murdered. There were tears in her eyes.

'She's trying to find her son,' one of the men among us said.

Half the group were scared and asked to go back.

'Stay together,' I told them, as they turned to retrace their steps.

Another one of the remaining group, a woman, had connected with the spirit.

'A man called William killed her and her baby,' she said. 'She just keeps saying: "Please give me my baby." '

My chest felt heavy. I wanted to cry. I was feeling the woman's sorrow. She was called Elizabeth and was so sad, it was hard to ignore her. We had to try to reunite her with her baby.

'Stand in a line and hold hands,' I said. 'Try to feel her energy.'

As we held hands and focused, a swirl of leaves surrounded us, moving slowly at first, but gathering momentum, whirling faster and faster, as we tried to connect with her baby. The rustling became louder and then we felt Thomas coming through – her son. He was only little, a skinny little thing, but as soon as she saw him they began running towards each other. We were all feeling their emotions – laughing and crying at the same time with the backdrop of leaves swirling around us. And then as they held each other, the leaves dropped all at once to the floor, like a curtain call, and the woman and her child were gone.

It was a poignant moment. Men and women in our group were crying and hugging each other. We'd done something special in reuniting a mother and son, and together they'd been able to find the light.

Back at the house, we did some research and found out that Elizabeth had been hung at the age of 28 after stealing some food to feed Thomas, six. After her death, she'd never left, waiting for her boy to join her. Now, at last, they were a little family again, and could find peace.

I've always found those encounters thrilling, if somewhat emotional at the time. But one night I arrived home and collapsed, exhausted, on the sofa. I would live half the time at Leigh's flat but still had my own house in Essex. I was so tired, I decided to have a bath and go to bed, and forgot to close myself down. As soon as I climbed under the duvet my eyes grew heavy and within seconds I was asleep.

When I woke up, I couldn't see anything, and I couldn't

breathe. Instantly, I knew why. Someone was lying on top of me, pinning me down. The weight was so heavy, it had to be a man.

'Get off me,' I muttered, struggling to speak. My ribcage felt like it was collapsing in on me. At the same time I instinctively raised my hands, ready to pummel the intruder – but there was nothing there. It was a spirit.

'I've left myself open,' I realized. It was like leaving your front door on the latch. Anyone could just barge in.

'Get off,' I screamed again, pushing an imaginary body away. Summoning all my strength, I jumped up. I didn't look back, but sprinted for the bedroom door, and ran down the stairs. I was dressed in my pyjamas and didn't stop to grab anything, except my handbag. I was gasping for breath, struggling for every bit of air. This was a panic attack, and I just needed to get away from that thing. It was menacing and brooding, and wanted to hurt me. I clattered out of the front door, desperately trying to find my car key in my bag, so I could jump straight in the driver's side and roar away. I left the front door open, all the lights on, but I didn't care what happened to the house or any of my stuff. I had to get away from that nasty spirit.

I rang Leigh on the way but he wasn't in. Luckily, I had a key to his flat, so could let myself in. Sitting, shaking on his sofa with all the lights on, I tried to take deep breaths and closed down all my chakras. I also did a cleansing spell to make sure every bit of that thing had gone, and then I sat waiting for Leigh to come home. He cuddled me, and calmed me down, but I couldn't sleep. It had made me feel that it was going to do something really nasty to me, and because I'd left myself open, the spirit had been able to threaten me physically. I'd felt him on top of me, been able to smell him. It was as real as if I'd woken up to find a real man there, and had reacted in the same way – the flight or fight state. I'd chosen to run, because I was too scared to do anything else. The next day I cleansed and smudged my house, and put protective crystals everywhere to keep him at bay. I never again went to bed without closing down all my chakras. That was a tough lesson learnt.

It isn't always the psychic who's shocked, though. Sometimes the spirits are the scared ones. While I was working at a psychic school in Bermuda, I took one group to an old derelict Baptist church near the Cambridge Beaches Hotel, where we were staying. It had caught my eye every time Leigh and I had driven past it, and so I knew it must be haunted.

The group included doctors, teachers and tourists of all nationalities, and we stood in a circle inside the abandoned church, trying to link with any energy present. We had to be careful when picking our way across the old rotten floorboards in the dark because some of the floor, and ceiling, had fallen through.

It was a gloriously starry night, and dust glinted in the light coming off our candles, all so different from a ghost hunt back home. Suddenly, the room felt dark, the candles began flickering and a really angry energy tore through the old church. A young man came through strongly and kept saying, 'Go and talk to my dad.' I could hear it and so could Louise, the spa manager in a hotel where I had previously stayed.

As his voice grew clearer he appeared – good-looking, with

walnut skin, and strong, handsome features. He looked about 19, and was thick-set and muscular. Louise started crying, and so did another girl, so I knew they could see him, too. Next to me, Darren, one of the men on the course, had goosebumps. I could feel the hairs on his arms standing up as his skin touched mine. It was 32 degrees outside but he was freezing.

The young man was furious because his life had been stolen. He was still unable to grasp that he was dead, it had all happened so fast.

'Go speak to my dad,' he kept pleading, and pointed towards the porchway of a house across the street.

The church didn't seem to have any light coming in now and was filled with a boggy stench, like stagnant water. It made me want to gag, and Louise was really sobbing. I could see why. The boy was standing right in front of her, his face aggressively tilted towards hers.

'It's OK,' I said, trying to soothe both of them. They were both so scared, although he was trying to hide his fear. The boy had been shot once by two men. He owed them money for drugs.

'I know I was silly,' he said. 'I wasn't heavily involved. I made a mistake.'

That was one mistake for which he'd paid the ultimate price. Now we sensed another energy, someone connected with the church.

'You are in God's place and you have no right.'

It was an old lady who had looked after the church when it was the bustling centre of the town. Now it had fallen into disrepair and she was angry. She was even more annoyed we were talking to the boy, who, she felt, had committed a sin.

'Leave here,' she ordered and we heard a bang. She was trying to make us leave, shutting doors and windows. Some of the group looked scared, and even I began to panic when I heard a police siren in the background.

'Let's go,' I urged, picking my way over the missing floorboards. It turned out the police weren't after us – how could they be? – but the sound of the siren was enough to spook even me.

Outside, one of the local women who'd come on the hunt confirmed that the boy we'd connected with had been shot by two men on a motorbike just a fortnight before with a single bullet to the chest at point blank range.

'His dad lives over there,' she said, pointing to a house with a verandah outside. I was tempted to visit the boy's father, but couldn't see what good it would do. He wanted justice, and I couldn't help him with that.

A couple of days later, a young woman came to see me for a reading, holding a baby. I knew who she was immediately. The boy's girlfriend and his four-month-old baby. He came through as soon as she sat down.

'He loves you,' I told her. 'He's sorry. He didn't want to leave you.'

His anger was still there, but the love for his family was stronger, and I was glad to put them in touch. She left smiling, and I felt sure he had found some kind of peace.

Of course, he had done something he shouldn't but he was young and didn't deserve to die over it. It was a tragedy that he had lost his life and a woman and baby had lost him forever. Nothing could bring him back, but to have heard from him, through me, meant everything to that woman. I was just happy to help.

13

Psychic to psychic

I couldn't take my eyes off him. It wasn't just his giant smile or the way he threw his head back when he laughed. John Edward was mesmerizing, even if it was through the small screen. I'd come across the American psychic on his TV show, 'Crossing Over', and tried to watch it every day. John was amazingly gifted, but what I loved about him was the natural way he dealt with the people he was giving messages to, and how he saw the kindness and humour in everything. His messages touched the loved ones he spoke to, but he didn't try to dress anything up. If the spirit he'd connected to said something in a funny or cheeky way, he told it how it was, but with a charm that made him a must-watch star.

'You could do that,' Leigh would tell me when he caught me watching John's show, but I wasn't so sure. It wasn't that I doubted my ability. I believed that Star and my guardian angels would always help me, and the spirits would come through to talk to their loved ones, but I'd never done anything on that kind of scale before. I'd stood on stage at the Spiritualist Church, and given group readings, which had always gone well, but that wasn't to thousands of people, as John did. I worked giving one-to-one readings, so that I could go into details and pass on a lot of information. Standing up in front of thousands was something else entirely.

John Edward was coming to London to perform at the Royal Albert Hall, so I got a ticket, and went along. He was even more incredible in real life than he was on TV. His talent, kindness and genuine star quality radiated out into the audience, capturing each and every one. That was something rare. I'd appeared on TV and had regular columns in magazines and newspapers, but how would I suddenly put on a huge show?

The next day I got my answer when Hilary Goldman called me unexpectedly, and invited me for lunch. She was Colin Fry's agent, and a TV producer. Colin was the equivalent of John Edward in the UK with his popular show, 'Sixth Sense'.

Someone else was already with Hilary when I arrived. She introduced herself but I didn't catch her name, too excited to be meeting Hilary. It was only when she excused herself to go to the ladies' that Hilary told me who she was – Meera Syal, who starred in 'The Kumars'. As usual, I didn't have a clue. I'm useless at spotting or recognizing celebrities, and had never watched the show, although I'd heard it was hilarious.

'Colin would love you to appear on his show,' Hilary said after Meera came back. 'And maybe you could join him on his tour?'

I agreed to pre-record a segment for Colin's show and think about going on tour. Then I gave Meera a reading. She was divorced, but she wouldn't be on her own for long.

'You've already met your next husband,' I said. 'He's already a friend. I can see you getting married and having a baby boy.'

She seemed happy with everything I told her, and she did go on to marry Sanjeev Bhaskar, who played her grandson in 'The Kumars', and they had a baby.

We began talking about how little I needed to know or see of someone to give them a reading. Hilary couldn't understand what I meant and just then I spotted a woman sat behind a screen at a table to the right of us. All I could see were her toes peeking out of her shoes, tucked under the table.

'I'll read her toes,' I said, immediately linking in to the woman's mother. She told me her daughter was divorcing her husband but was feeling guilty because she'd met another man whom she believed was her soul mate. In fact, her mother had engineered the meeting, and was really pleased with herself, but her daughter felt she shouldn't get involved again until her divorce came through.

'It's a dilemma for her, and causing her some real heartache,' I said.

Just then the woman's toes moved, and her head poked around the screen.

'Are you talking about me?' she asked, and I nodded. I must have been talking too loudly, and could hardly lie about it now.

'You're besotted with this new guy,' I told her. 'Your mum's here and says he's perfect for you and not to feel guilty.'

The woman blinked, a bit shocked, but wanted to know more.

'Everything you've said is spot on,' she admitted, and I grinned at Hilary.

'See, toes never lie,' I said.

A couple of weeks later, I went to watch Colin film his show in the studio. It was fascinating to watch how he worked. He was a gentle man with an amazing gift, and very humble. Hilary, Colin and I went for lunch afterwards and he was great company, but he never spoke about himself. He was ego-free. I liked him and couldn't wait to appear on his show. He'd arranged for me to see a woman at her house with the film crew.

'How will you get there?' Colin asked as we left the restaurant.

'In my car, of course,' I said, pointing to it. Colin burst out laughing. It had been my birthday just a few weeks earlier and Leigh had bought me the personalized number plate TAROT as a present.

'That's genius,' Colin said as I explained how the number plate had read T17 until Leigh had got an extra screw put in to make the numbers look like an A. He and his friend, the psychic Tony Stockwell, who used to tour the country with him, always called me Tarot after that, and the name stuck.

'Have fun filming,' Colin said. 'See you on the show.'

So off I went to Julie's house. She had the most beautiful, big house in the country, but she didn't use two of the bedrooms, some outhouses, a patio area or a conservatory because she said they had a bad feeling. She also said that her 14-year-old daughter couldn't sleep, and when she did, she had nightmares that were so vivid they left her sobbing and traumatised.

'We think the house is haunted,' Julie said. 'We need your help.'

Already, I could sense a brooding, male energy in the house. It was the original owner, from 200 years ago. He was angry because Julie wanted to make drastic alterations to 'his' home.

'He says you're going to cut down his oak tree,' I told her. 'That's why he's so mad. He says you can't touch it, and he won't leave while it's under threat.'

Julie admitted they'd thought about cutting down the tree and doing a lot of building work in and outside the house.

'He's angry because his wife is buried in the garden,' I told her. 'You can't disturb her grave. He won't let you.'

Julie didn't want to upset him, and promised not to touch the tree or his wife's grave.

'I just want my daughter to be left in peace,' she said, and so we agreed that she wouldn't touch the tree or the garden. The spirit seemed to accept her promises, and instantly the intense, negative feeling around parts of the house and pool area lifted.

Julie's friend Pauline had joined us and wanted a reading, and was also eager to be on Colin's show. I didn't want to talk just about the ghost and the house, though. Pauline had lost her father, and I'd asked her to give me something of his to hold during the reading. She handed me his gold watch, and I connected with him straightaway.

'Your dad can't get a word in edgeways and lets your mum do all the talking for him,' I said.

Pauline nodded and said her dad had suffered from a bad stammer, so had always been quiet.

'Mum's a right chatterbox,' I said, and the image of a cameo popped into my mind.

'I had a thing about cameos when I was younger,' Pauline said, 'and so they bought me a matching ring and necklace.'

We chatted for a little bit longer, and once we'd finished filming, I cleansed and smudged the house. Then I placed protective crystals all around it to energize it and stop Julie's daughter feeling traumatised. The reading was shown the following month on the show, and Julie and Pauline were delighted to be on TV, and that the ghost had stopped giving a bad vibe in the house.

After that, I was asked to do a photoshoot and met the queen of psychic TV herself, Sally Morgan. We both wrote columns for *Spirit & Destiny* magazine.

The photoshoot was in a studio in London, and Sally was in the middle of having her photo taken when I arrived. While I was having my make-up done, I chatted to her husband, John, who is now a star in his own right after appearing on her reality TV show, 'Psychic Sally On The Road'. John's lovely, and we were nattering away. Sally came straight over as soon as the camera stopped clicking, and gave me a hug.

'How are you, darling?' she asked. 'Do you have time to give me a reading?'

I almost laughed. Here was the biggest psychic star in Britain, and she was asking me to read her Tarot. I was flattered, and asked the make-up lady to wait while I went off with Sally for a few minutes. I was shuffling my cards in a small back room when she said, 'I've got your mum here, Jayne.' I didn't doubt her, but she began to tell me things only Mum would know, and I must admit I did feel a bit teary.

'She's so proud of you,' Sally said, and I swallowed. 'She thinks you could do what I do.'

I laughed at that. Trust Mum to tell Sally Morgan I could do a stage show, too! I gave Sally a Tarot reading, which was all about how she was going to be even more successful and do more TV work, and then I began thinking about Mum's message. Why not do a stage show? What did I have to lose? So I organized one at Littlecote House Hotel in Hungerford. It was to be small and intimate, since it was my first one, for just over 100 people. I wasn't ready for the O2 yet!

On the night, I wasn't nervous. Just before I went on, I opened myself up and linked in straightaway with a woman, so I knew a spirit was already there to give a message to someone in the audience. I've never failed to link in with Spirit, so didn't think I would disappoint anyone who'd come to see me. Star would never let me down. But it was a two-hour show, so I decided to do what Colin Fry does and work in tandem with another psychic. He always appeared with Tony Stockwell, and I decided to go on stage with one of the Psychic Sisters, Nina Ashby. When one of us had a message to pass over, we'd step forward and the other would step back, then we'd swap over. Now I took a deep breath, and stepped out in front of the audience.

'I've got a woman here who connected with me backstage,' I said. 'She was very suicidal and, sorry to have to say this, but she died at her own hands.'

I described the woman – slender, in her thirties, and very pretty – but no one took the message. I could feel a noose tightening around my neck, so I knew she'd hanged herself. I passed on as much information as was tactful, but still no one claimed her, and after five minutes, I had to move on. But the woman didn't leave. She stayed with me, waiting for a chance to give her message.

'She says she's sorry,' I said. 'She wants to talk to her sister.' I looked around the room, at all the women, but no one seemed to know who the woman was. 'She wants you to know she's safe,' I said, desperate to connect this spirit with her loved one. Nothing. I didn't understand it. The message was so strong and clear – why wasn't anyone there to receive it?

It was an emotional evening. Hungerford is the town where 27-year-old Michael Robert Ryan went berserk, going on a shooting spree and murdering sixteen people and injuring fifteen more before killing himself. Six of his victims came through to talk to their loved ones. It was harrowing and uplifting at the same time, and at the end of the evening, I was shattered.

I'd probably passed on around forty messages over the two hours, and was very pleased that my first stage show had gone without a hitch. A few members of the audience wanted to meet me to say thanks for their messages, and we ended up chatting and hugging, and I tried to comfort the people who were crying, not able to believe they'd heard from their loved ones.

But all the time the woman was still there, hoping to pass on her message. Why hadn't she been able to connect? It was a mystery I was desperate to solve. I didn't have long to wait. The next day, a woman who was meant to be attending the psychic development weekend just starting at Littlecote, rang up to say she wasn't coming.

'I'm so sorry,' she said. 'I was on my way to the hotel but my car broke down.'

She had to ring the AA to tow her back home, and on the way received a call to tell her to get there quickly because something awful had happened to her sister. She found out that, tragically, her sister had killed herself the night before – just before I went onstage. The woman had been in the audience, watching me give out the message, but hadn't known what her sister had done. Now she had to identify her sister's body. It was a terrible story, and I felt so sorry for her.

She came on the next psychic weekend we ran at the hotel, and was the most lovely woman. I was able to pass on the entire message from her sister, which meant a lot to her. She turned out to be a gifted psychic, who could read auras brilliantly, and has since linked in to her sister, and found peace with what she did and understood why.

Those circumstances were so unusual. I think the woman's sister must have known that she was coming to the psychic development weekend and tried to get the message straight to her, like making a phone call, but was too quick. The woman didn't realize the message was for her, because she didn't know that her sister had killed herself.

I'm a magnet for unrested spirits. It's as if they look in the psychic or medium phone book and see me listed under clairvoyant for most desperate souls. I do tend to attract an unusual amount of suicide and murder victims, or mentally and physically abused spirits. In fact, I see that as my purpose really. That's what Star spent all my childhood and teenage years preparing me for. She knew I would have a special ability to help those spirits and their loved ones, and it can be so rewarding.

One woman came to see me in Epping, and handed me a mobile phone.

'It was my son's,' she said, 'but it doesn't work.'

I took the phone from her and instantly connected with her son, who was around 26, olive skinned and very, very handsome. I could tell that he took his own life, but at first I couldn't see how. He was hunched over in a clearing in a forest or woodland, and then I sensed that his body had been like that for three months.

'You couldn't find him,' I told her and her eyes filled with tears. He had broken up with his girlfriend and had a baby. His life had meant nothing after they'd left, and he'd fallen into debt. 'He couldn't see a way out,' I told his mum, who was crying now. 'Every day he became more and more depressed and overwhelmed by the situation.'

She had tried everything to find her missing son, and it had been awful for her not knowing what had happened to him. So it had been a kind of release when a man had come across her son's body while walking his dog. But the body had been so badly decayed she didn't know how he had died, and didn't feel she had closure. I held the mobile phone in both hands and focused. I could see her son taking tablets.

'He died from an overdose of painkillers,' I said, and she broke down.

'Thank you,' she kept saying. 'I just wanted to know.'

She also wanted help in getting his mobile phone started, but it had been outside in the damp forest too long and couldn't be fixed.

'There aren't any answers in here,' I said. 'He's beside you now and is sorry, but he didn't know what to do.'

He loved his mother and just kept apologizing. It had all become too much for him, and he'd taken that way out. If only he'd been able to confide in his mum, he would have been happy again in time. That's the awful thing about suicide. It's a decision that can't be taken back, and damages so many lives. Mostly, the mothers come to see me, and when they are so hurt by their children's suicide, like this woman, I give them healing. It's not enough but it dulls some of the pain for a while, and it's all I can do to help them. I can give them messages from their lost ones, and give them healing to try to soothe the hurt, but I can't bring their loved ones back, no matter how much I wish I could.

One time in Bermuda, we did something very special for a grieving mother. Her son, who was 10, appeared in one of the psychic development classes I was holding. I could see him very clearly, and interrupted a class to say he was there, and he was crying for his mum. No one answered me, and so I described him.

'He is called Joseph and is asking for candy,' I said. Still no one claimed him. The boy, who was in the corner sobbing, was demanding strawberry candy.

'He wants hard sweets, not soft,' I said, repeating exactly what he was saying. Finally, a woman put up her hand.

'My son was called Joseph,' she said. 'He was killed on the

way to the shop to get strawberry candy.'

I stopped her from saying any more. I wanted the group to try to link in to how he died, so we could validate he was there. I closed my eyes and saw a bus careering towards me. Joseph had been about to step out to cross the road to the candy store when a red bus smashed into him, killing him instantly. His mother was now 52 and said it had happened around twenty years earlier, but she'd never stopped missing him.

'It still hurts every day,' she said, hot tears falling.

I could see him so strongly, and wanted her to know he was there.

'Let's get in a line,' I told the group, 'and touch the person in front on the shoulders.' Then I asked Joseph's mum to stand in the middle, so she would feel all the energy from the group.

'Try to see, smell and touch Joseph,' I told everyone, and they all focused, and began to sway. Suddenly, the room filled up with the sweet scent of candy and the distinct smell of a boy.

'I can smell him,' his mum said, shocked. 'For the first time, I can smell my boy.'

I wanted her to touch him, so brought the line over to the corner, where he was still standing.

'Try bouncing your hand off his aura,' I told her. 'Just keep moving over this space until you feel him.' She swiped the air for a few minutes, and then she stopped. Her hand paused, and she let out a cry.

'Joseph,' she said as her hand felt his outline.

He embraced her. It was strange because most people couldn't see him, so she looked as though she was cuddling the air, but she was touching her son, and it was an amazing thing. She was crying and so was he as they were physically reunited. Everyone in the room was so happy that they'd maybe helped in some way, and Joseph was so much happier after being in his mum's arms one more time.

'I've waited years for that,' she said, wiping her tears. 'But it was worth every day just to feel my son again.'

That's the thing about love. You can lose a loved one, and the overwhelming grief that stops the world turning for a while can ease, but the pain is always there, just below the surface. Months, years and even decades can pass, but a mother's heart and arms still ache for her lost child, and a wife still longs for one last kiss with her husband.

Children suffer terribly when a parent passes over. One grieving daughter came to see me in Essex. In her late twenties, she was very elegant, dressed in a white blouse, black blazer and skirt and court shoes. Everything about her was immaculate. Her highlighted hair was perfect, as was her 'barely there' make-up.

When she sat opposite me for her reading, her dad came through, telling me to lift up the sleeves of her blouse. Normally, I would have said the message out loud, but this time, for some reason, I reached across and pulled back her cuffs. There wasn't anything there and the woman pulled her arms back, shocked.

'What are you doing?' she demanded, furious. Her dad answered.

'You need to lift her sleeves higher,' he said. There something about him that made me trust what he was saying, so I told her he was asking me to look at her arms.

'He's asking what you're hiding,' I said, reaching out for her arms. She eyed me, then slid her right arm across the table. I lifted the sleeve higher and paused. Bright red scars criss-crossed her forearm where she'd dug a knife or razor blade over and over into her flesh.

'Why are you self-harming?' I asked gently. 'Your dad wants to know.'

The woman broke down, and explained she didn't know how to deal with her grief since her father had died of pancreatic cancer. She'd been hurting so much, she'd found release in slashing at her own flesh until it bled. For her, it was some kind of physical manifestation of the pain she felt inside about losing him. It made total sense, but was so sad.

'You've got to stop,' I told her. 'Your dad wants to see his grandson born.'

For the first time, the woman smiled. She explained that she'd been thinking about trying for a baby, but still felt so guilty about getting married so soon after her father's funeral.

'He would have wanted you to be happy,' I said, but guilt shrouded the woman.

'I just miss him,' she said, bursting into tears, and I reached across and held her hand. She was hurting so much, I had to help her. So I sat and talked to her for a couple of hours, and she admitted that on the way to the reading, she had thought about jumping under a train.

'I just want this awful feeling to stop,' she said. 'I don't know how to be happy without Dad.'

I hugged her then, so sorry that she didn't know how to cope with her grief. They'd been so close she couldn't handle life without her dad. I gave her some healing, and made her promise to seek some professional counselling to stop her from self-harming or doing anything silly.

'Your dad wants you to enjoy life, like he did,' I said, and she nodded.

After she left, I really felt as though she'd come to me that day for a reason, which was to get permission from her dad to stop grieving. She'd been so down, she'd even been suicidal, but that's not what he would have wanted. He wanted her to be happy with her new husband, and to have a family, so she could love raising a child as much as he'd loved watching her grow up.

Three months later, she came back to see me and looked much better.

'I wanted to say thank you for your kindness,' she said. Then she undid her jacket, and patted her stomach. There was the tiny bulge of a baby bump.

'Congratulations,' I said, grinning. 'Your dad is going to be ecstatic.'

Just over six months later, I opened a letter, and a picture of her with a newborn baby son fell out. She looked transformed, a tired but contented mother with her baby in her arms.

'You saved my life,' she'd written. 'Now I'm getting on with living.'

It was the sweetest thing I'd ever read.

 *14*

Coming to America

This was going to be tricky. Should I skirt around the issue or just come straight out and say it? 'No point changing the habit of a lifetime,' I thought, staring at the charismatic man sitting in front of me. He had salt and pepper hair, and a gentle air about him, and was so polite, I winced as I opened my mouth.

'You're going to leave your wife,' I said. 'It's not that you're unhappy, but it's because you've met your soul mate.' I looked across the table at my client, waiting for a reaction. He just looked at me.

'Your father is here,' I said, glad to be laying the blame for such honesty somewhere else. His father had come through as soon as he had sat down for his reading. Now he was telling me how his son had met his soul mate on a recent trip to New York. 'You should be with her, your dad's saying,' I told him. 'She's The One.' I also told him that her name was Jennifer, and described her – petite, with long dark hair, and really beautiful. The man's eyes widened, but he quickly composed himself.

Luckily, his dad had plenty of other news, mostly about business opportunities and film work his son was involved in. His son was an actor – I later discovered he'd starred in the film 'The Bank Job' with Jason Statham – and film producer.

'Thank you,' the man said at the end of the reading, handing me his business card.

His name was Alki David, and in his line of work, he obviously had TV contacts. I had been thinking about trying to get my own TV show for a while now. I'd appeared as a guest on so many other psychics' shows, along with mainstream programmes such as 'The Graham Norton Show' and 'Trisha'. I was different from Colin Fry and Sally Morgan, so why shouldn't I give it a shot? Maybe Alki could help me. I didn't know him, but for some reason I did feel a deep connection with him. And he had given me his business card, hadn't he? Why do that if you didn't want people to call you? So I rang his number. I thought I might get his secretary or a voice message, but he answered.

'I'm Jayne Wallace,' I began.

'The psychic,' he interrupted, and I smiled.

'Yes, I was wondering if you could help me.'

Alki seemed genuinely pleased to hear from me and told me to come to his Film On offices a couple of weeks later so we could talk. When I got there, he told me that he'd been surprised at how accurate my reading was. He'd also listened to his father's advice. After our reading, he'd literally gone straight home, packed a bag and left his wife, Emma. He'd got on a plane and flown from London to New York. I tried not to feel guilty. I didn't decide these things. How could I? And it was his dad in spirit who actually told him, I consoled myself. I was just the messenger. I didn't even know Alki. But I'd seen that he would be happy with this new woman, Jennifer.

After talking over his and my ideas for TV shows, he said he would look into how he could help me, and promised to get in touch with his American contacts. Then I offered to give Alki another reading. Straightaway I linked in to his father again.

'Jennifer is your soul mate,' I reiterated, and Alki smiled. 'And I see an engagement ring, a wedding ...' I went on, 'and children ... and you'll be moving to the US to be together.' I smiled, glad to see him look so happy.

After the reading, Alki asked Leigh and me to dinner. Jennifer had accompanied him to London and would be there, too. I was so excited to meet her, having seen her so clearly in that first reading for Alki. After that, we kept in touch, speaking nearly every day, some weeks, and our friendship grew. It didn't ever feel like psychic and client – of course, I gave Alki advice if he ever asked me, but everything between us always felt mutual. And although he told me he was very wealthy – a shipping billionaire, in fact – none of that mattered. He was my mate.

Soon I received a call from Alki asking Leigh and me to fly to Los Angeles.

'I've got some meetings lined up for you with TV executives,' Alki said.

Leigh and I decided to combine it with a holiday, but couldn't believe how hospitable Alki was being. He'd arranged our stay at a gorgeous hotel in Santa Monica, and he'd lined up several auditions with top TV contacts.

'He trusts you,' Leigh said as we settled into our seats on the aeroplane.

Leigh was really looking forward to seeing Alki again and catching up – they'd got on really well when they'd met at dinner in London. I knew our trip was important, too, because this was one of those rare times when I felt Mum's presence. I've felt her maybe four times in my life since she passed, and this was one of those visits.

'I'm so lucky, Mum,' I confided as I looked out of the window, and watched England disappearing under the clouds. Not only had I put Alki and others in touch with their lost loved ones, but I'd got to know some incredibly kind people, who often became my friends. It felt as though Mum was always helping me by sending the right people into my life just when I needed them. 'Thank you,' I whispered, closing my eyes and savouring the loving sensation of her around me.

I'd had so many opportunities thanks to my psychic ability, including travelling and seeing places I could only otherwise have dreamt about. This time, as well as seeing Alki, and talking to the TV people, I'd arranged to drop in on a famous actress client of mine, who lived in LA. Usually, I saw her in London, but she was in Hollywood to make a new film.

'It's brilliant to see you,' she said, welcoming me into her home, which was like something out of a glossy magazine, but then she was an A-list star. What I loved about her was that, even though she was world famous, she was incredibly down-to-earth. People might think it's easy to get sucked into the fame thing, but most of the superstar clients I saw were remarkably normal. Some could still surprise me, though. One day a woman phoned to say that her boss wanted a reading.

'He's a very sensitive, private man,' she explained. 'So he won't want anyone to know he's consulting you.' I smiled. Most of my clients demanded confidentiality, so that was nothing new. 'Can you give him a reading over the phone in a week's time?' she asked.

We arranged the exact date and time, and my fee. Then I waited for my phone to ring. The woman called at exactly the time we'd arranged.

'I have my boss here,' she said, and then she said his name. I paused for a second, and had to check that I hadn't misheard.

'Did you say ..?' I said, repeating the name. She confirmed that she had, and I had to take a deep breath. I'm not normally starstruck but this was a global superstar. I'd been to see him in concert at Wembley and had all his albums. I couldn't believe I was going to speak to him. But I pulled myself together. 'Be professional,' I told myself. 'Don't act any differently.' In a split second, I forced myself to dissociate the man from his public persona. The fan in me wanted to scream 'Wow, ohmigod' and be excited, but Jayne Wallace, the psychic was stronger.

'Fine, I'm ready,' I said, as if I was taking a call from my bank manager, and clicked into work mode. It was a conference call and the man's voice was faint. He and his PA were in the same room, but as I linked in to Spirit and got ready to give his reading, he asked her to leave. The man was going through a lot of difficulties surrounding his childhood and upbringing, and was emotionally vulnerable. I could tell he was lonely, even though he was one of the most famous men on the planet, and that filled me with sadness. He found it hard to trust anyone, and even harder to relax away from work. He was about to start a world tour and wanted to know if he was strong enough for the gruelling regime.

'It's going to be tough on you,' I said. 'You're very weak physically and mentally, and you need to recharge your batteries so you're strong enough.'

He had a gentle energy, and was filled with pain and tears. I didn't think that he even wanted to do the world tour; he just didn't seem to have a choice. I didn't understand why, but every time I linked in to him, I was overwhelmed with sadness.

The reading lasted for almost an hour, and he didn't ask any questions about anything but his tour. It was worrying him a lot, and I tried to give him ways to prepare mentally and physically. It was almost like dealing with a child, his aura and energy were so fragile. I was very honoured to have read for him, and hoped I'd helped him, even in a small way. I was shocked to discover that he'd passed over not long afterwards. I connected with him in Spirit and was relieved to discover he was happier and stronger. His worries had disappeared, although he will never be forgotten. His talent was too huge for that.

I was one of millions around the world who grieved for him. But I was busy. I had TV executives to see. They all seemed very interested in talking to me and hearing Alki's and my ideas, but it was 2009, and the recession was biting in the media.

'We love you,' they all said, 'but we don't have any money to try anything new right now.'

I didn't let it get to me. We were having an amazing time in LA, although we didn't get to go out with Jennifer because she was so busy designing her new swimwear line. That had to wait until we were all back in London, where she looked just as amazing as ever, and jumped up to hug me in the restaurant. I loved watching Jen and Alki together, the way they looked at each other, and their chemistry. It was obvious they were meant to be together, but it went deeper than just attraction. They were spiritually connected. Looking at them made me smile.

'They're going to get married and have babies,' I told Leigh. He grinned.

'Well make sure you're their bridesmaid,' he joked. 'Without you they might not even be together.'

We laughed about it, but I knew it was nothing to do with me really. Alki and Jennifer grew closer, and he spent more time in New York to be with her.

'I've found a house I like in Beverley Hills,' he said one time when he called. 'I'm sending you some photographs. Should I buy it?'

As he described it, nestling in the hills, it sounded amazing, but he wanted to renovate it, and take out the old pool and put in a new one.

'Shall I do this?' he asked, and I clicked on my laptop to look at the photos he'd sent. A gorgeous, huge house filled my computer screen. Not only was it beautiful, but it had a good vibe about it. I could tell he would be happy there.

'It's a good house,' I told him. 'Buy it.'

Then I got a call from a TV company in England to make a pilot for a prospective show, to be called 'Psychic Salon'. A film crew had to follow me 24/7 as I gave readings to various people, including celebrities. I met finalists from 'X Factor', and gave readings to Tricia from Pineapple Dance Studios and Tina

Barrett from S Club 7. It was fun.

During the filming, Alki phoned to say he and Jen were on their way to meet me on location. Jennifer looked radiant, and I soon saw why. She was wearing the biggest diamond ring I had ever seen – a stunning black diamond.

'How did I miss that before?' I laughed, hugging her and Alki. 'Congratulations.'

'I have something to ask you,' Jennifer said. 'Will you be my bridesmaid?' I looked from one to the other and realized they were serious.

'Yes please,' I responded. 'That's fantastic news.'

They were set to get married in May 2010 in Oheka Castle in New York. Oheka Castle has an amazing ambience, with beautiful stone carvings and ceilings that almost hit the sky. I was to be one of eight bridesmaids along with a flower girl and two page boys.

Like any bride, Jennifer was soon making wedding plans, and chose luscious silk dresses for us in deep violet.

When Jennifer walked in, wearing her designer wedding dress, I gasped. She was stunning.

'You look beautiful,' I whispered, tears threatening to spill. The style of the dress was pure fairytale – floor-length white silk studded with hundreds of sparkling crystals, showing off her fabulous curves – and she'd chosen a matching crystal tiara for her headdress. I know I'm biased, but I honestly felt she was the most beautiful bride I'd ever seen.

It was an emotional wedding, and managed to feel intimate, even though it was one of the celebrity weddings of the year.

I swallowed, watching Alki and Jennifer take their vows. They looked so happy, and it was breathtaking. Afterwards, we enjoyed a lavish banquet in the opulent dining room and watched them cut their six-foot tall, four-tier cake, festooned with white flowers and tiny crystals.

'How do you know the couple?' one of the guests on our table asked me.

'Oh, just from around,' I said casually, daring Leigh to say anything. I was proud to have been there from the beginning and to have realized what they had was so special.

I was happy, too. I had Leigh, my family, good friends and my gift. Back home, I had back-to-back readings, and one of the women who came to see me was artist Tracey Emin. She'd hit the headlines with her installations 'My Bed' –her bed covered with everyday objects, such as her worn knickers – and 'Everyone I Have Ever Slept With' – a tent embroidered with the names of everyone she has slept with. She was controversial, in your face, and I liked her. But sitting across from her at Selfridges, she didn't look too happy. Her father came through straightaway but Tracey didn't want to connect with him.

'It's my nan,' she insisted, but I could tell a woman from a man, even if the person was dead.

'No, it's your dad,' I said, but she wouldn't listen.

I work by linking in to Spirit and passing on messages from there. Tracey's father talked about things that had happened in the past to try to convince her he was really there, but she didn't want that kind of reading. She was more interested in knowing what was going to happen in the future than dwelling on the past, but I didn't operate like that.

'Maybe you should see one of the other girls,' I suggested. One of the other Psychic Sisters, Geraldine, was also an astrologer, so she could do predictions, and Tracey agreed to see her instead.

'Sorry, I can't read you,' I said, but there were no hard feelings from my side. I thought she was lovely and incredibly talented. I was sure Tracey wasn't impressed with me, so didn't expect to hear from her again, although I thought I might see her around Selfridges since a concept store 'Walking Around My World' with items selected by Tracey from throughout the store along with her prints and merchandise, was about to open in Selfridges' Wonder Room.

I was surprised when I heard that she had listed the Psychic Sisters as one of her favourite six things in the department store. That meant we were invited to have a stand at her exhibition, so we could offer visitors readings, and Tracey also asked us to be at the press launch. I went along with two of the girls, Gemma and Nina, for what we called a 'mix and mingle'. We would walk around the party and give readings to anyone who wanted them. It was a small gathering of around fifty journalists, and I offered crystal readings, for which guests picked three crystals out of a bag. I hadn't been there long when I bumped into Tracey.

'Do you want a reading?' I asked her, expecting her to refuse. But she quickly picked out her crystals, and waited for me to predict her future. Her dad was standing beside her at the party, but yet again she insisted it was her nan. So I tried to ignore Star and my spirit guides and focused on the three crystals she'd chosen – a blue lace agate for artistic talent and creative passion; a rose quartz, for relationships; and a tiger's eye. Usually, this was for protection, but in Tracey's case it told me she was incredibly spiritual and intuitive at a very high level. Her artistic ability included the most amazing sixth sense.

'Come to the after party,' Tracey said. 'It's upstairs and will be fun.'

So as the launch party came to a close, I followed her up to Hicks restaurant, where tables were laden with food and bottles of champagne.

'Will you do readings at my birthday party?' she asked. It was to be at her studio in East London in three weeks.

'I'll be there,' I smiled.

It was funny that Tracey was booking me, even though I'd never been able to finish a reading for her. But I was happy to go along and meet her friends. Stephen Fry was there and designer Vivienne Westwood, along with many artists. I went around chatting to guests, and asking them if they wanted readings. The evening flew by.

Tracey was having a great time, and as she and I stood chatting, I realized what a funny, intelligent woman she is.

'Give me your car keys,' she said suddenly. 'Come on, I'll give you a reading.'

I couldn't say no to that, and handed over the keys to my BMW. Tracey held the keyring, and was unbelievable.

'There are eight of you in your family,' she said, and I nodded. I have seven brothers and sisters. 'Your dad says you're going to America, where you'll be incredibly successful.' I shrugged. I'd already been there and hadn't had any luck so far, but Tracey was adamant. 'You'll be big over there one day,' she said. 'But right now, you're going to have to move your concession in Selfridges.'

I shook my head. Psychic Sisters had been there for 6 years and had no plans to move. Tracey smiled.

'You wait and see,' she said, and I laughed. She was so confident, I almost believed her.

The reading was brief – only about ten minutes – but it was so detailed I was impressed.

'You can always get a job with me if being an artist doesn't work out,' I teased her and she laughed. But it was late and I needed to get off.

'I've had a brilliant time,' I said. 'Happy Birthday.' She hugged me.

'Wait there,' she said. 'I've got a present for you.' It was her birthday, and she was giving me a present. She soon came rushing back.

'This is for you,' she said, handing me a print. It was a pencil drawing of two shoes with a rude message underneath.

'Is this really for me?' I said, stunned. Tracey nodded, and I left, clutching my present. It's now hanging in my bedroom, and every morning when I wake up, I smile when I read what Tracey wrote: 'You can't fuck a shoe'. It's typical Tracey – mad, creative and inspiring. I'm very proud to have met her.

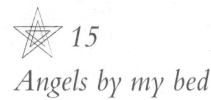

15

Angels by my bed

As soon as I woke up, I registered an uneasy feeling in my stomach. It wasn't a pain as such – more a premonition, the gut instinct everyone says you should listen to. I could actually feel when something was going to happen, but this time I wanted it to go away. I wasn't in the mood for a prediction, especially if it was bad news.

I glanced over to the other side of my bedroom where my suitcase stood packed and ready to go. I was off to the Maldives on holiday with my brother Mark, and four of our friends. We'd been saving up for what seemed like forever, and I couldn't wait to go. I was tired, and needed to feel the sun on my body and swollen joints. It had been a while since I'd been away, so I wasn't about to listen to any bad feeling in my stomach.

Instead, I jumped in the shower, dressed, checked that I had my passport and waited for the taxi to show up. We'd been planning this trip for so long, and had booked to do a Padi diving course. My consultant was dead against it. He'd refused to sign my medical papers but I was determined to get my diving certificate, no matter what. I wasn't going to let my rheumatoid arthritis stop me from having fun, or going on adventures. 'You only live once,' Mum used to say, and so, stubborn as ever, I'd vowed to dive anyway.

I had been excited, but after waking up with this funny feeling, I wasn't so sure. Every time I imagined diving, my body gave an involuntary shudder. Was that what my queasy tummy was about? I paused for a moment and connected with Star.

'Be careful,' she said, and I felt sick. Was something bad going to happen while I was diving?

'No,' I muttered, shaking my head. I was going to have a good time. I'd been looking forward to it for ages. I wouldn't take any risks, but no one, not even Star, was going to stop me from doing this.

'The taxi's here,' Mark shouted, and I threw my case in the back.

'Paradise here we come,' I said, ignoring my icky tummy.

The flight was long, and we were all exhausted by the time we arrived, but it was worth the journey. Our island, ringed by a powdery white beach, was lush with vegetation, and water bungalows jutted over an azure sea.

'Am I dreaming?' I asked, blinking. I'd never seen anywhere so beautiful. The brochure didn't do it justice.

'Let's go for a dip,' I said, and we all dumped our bags in our bungalow and I changed into my new white bikini. The sea was warm, like a bath, and so clear I could see straight to the sand below, and watch schools of tiny fishes dart in between my legs.

'This is the life,' I sighed, laying back in the water and floating on my back. I closed my eyes, feeling the gentle waves lap my body, and the sun on my face. I began to let my mind wander, opening up and beginning to meditate. Then I heard a voice.

It was Star. Connecting with her, I had that sick feeling in my stomach again. She had something important to tell me, and I wasn't sure I wanted to listen to it. I took a deep breath, steeling myself.

'Jayne!' My brother's voice sliced through my thoughts. I jumped up, instantly disconnecting with Star.

'What?' I yelled, and he said he was going snorkelling.

'Wait for me,' I shouted, wading through the shallow water. This was my dream holiday and I wanted to see and do as much as possible. So I caught up with him and the others, and was soon swimming under the water alongside the most colourful fish. It was like being in the film *Finding Nemo*, and I was soon lost in exploring everything to do with our island.

We had two days to fill before we started the diving course, which was full-on for a week, and were keen to pack in as much as we could. Every time I paused, I felt Star nagging at me, trying to get me to connect and listen to her, but I wanted a break from her and my psychic life. I was exhausted and needed to recharge my batteries, so I didn't burn myself out. I'd been working flat out and wanted a rest.

I hardly ever got any time to myself. Don't get me wrong, I love being a psychic and being able to connect people with their loved ones in Spirit, but it's not a job. It's a 24/7 responsibility, and whenever I told anyone what I did, they would ask for a reading, or try to get me to guess what they were thinking or about to do. It was tiring. For once, I just wanted to be able to close my eyes, and, like everyone else, not be bombarded with messages. So I closed myself off, and made sure nothing came through, not even Star.

I needed to focus on my Padi course, which was really difficult because the English-speaking instructor was ill. We were taught by two Italian instructors instead, who didn't speak English. So instead of listening to lectures from them, we had to watch videos in English, and make sure we knew enough to pass our theory exams. It was a hard week, but I kept myself going with the thought of being able to go out and dive under the ocean.

In the meantime, we went on shallow dives to practise what we'd learnt in class, but I didn't know I had to 'equalize' – pinch my nose and blow so that my ears popped. No one had mentioned it to me, and soon I had a splitting headache and a ringing in my ears. Each day I expected it to get easier, but by the fourth day, my earache was so bad, I couldn't dive and my chest hurt. I went to lay down on my bed, but winced with every breath. It felt like I'd been kicked in the ribs, and the pain grew stronger and stronger.

After a few hours, I was crying. Stabbing pains tore through my chest every time I breathed in or exhaled. I was taking shallow breaths to try to minimize the pain, but then I felt faint, and feared I was going to pass out.

'Help me,' I gasped when Mark came to check on me. He felt my forehead and shook his head. 'You're burning up, Sis,' he said. 'I'm going to call a doctor.'

I should have let him, but I thought it was just a chest infection, which would go if I took some painkillers. Besides, I didn't want to ruin everyone's holiday, so I swallowed some tablets and waited for it to pass. It grew worse. Soon, my lungs were making a bubbling noise whenever I took a breath. Our friend Lisa joined Mark and decided I needed to be seen. I tried to protest, but couldn't speak the pain was so bad.

'I'm going to be sick,' I gasped and ran into the bathroom. I sat on the edge of the bath, and gasped for air. Then I splashed my face with cold water, and tried to calm down. The sickness subsided, but the pain was slicing through me. Trying not to cry, I rubbed my ribs.

'I wanted to warn you,' a voice said. It was Star. I should have listened to her. This was my fault. I'd refused to take her warning, and now I was ill.

Suddenly, as I sat there, waiting for Star to give me her 'I told you so' speech, a surge of heat rushed through me. I gasped, and then realized my pain had almost gone. Instead of telling me off, Star had given me healing. I took a deep breath and my lungs didn't feel on fire any more.

'Thank you,' I whispered and went back into my bedroom. Lisa, Mark and two men were standing there.

'We found a group of doctors visiting from Male,' Lisa said, relieved to see I was looking a bit better. One of the men was carrying his doctor's bag. He took my temperature and listened to my chest and back with a stethoscope.

'I think you've got fluid on your lungs,' he said, 'and a nasty ear infection.'

He wanted me to go to hospital, but the nearest one was two hours away in the capital, Male. I shook my head. I was genuinely feeling better, and didn't want to go to a foreign hospital on my own.

'I'll be fine,' I insisted, and the doctor made me promise to eat some soup and get some rest. 'I will come and check on you again before we leave for the mainland,' he said.

I did as I was told, and sipped some clear soup, which was delicious, and then huddled under the covers. I was so tired I was soon asleep.

Next thing I knew, screams filled my ears, and made my head throb. They were so loud, my whole body shook. I snapped my eyes open, desperate to find out who was screaming like that. Then I realized it was me. Star's healing had worn off, and I was in agony. My lungs felt like a knife had been punched clean through them, and I was struggling to breathe. Tears replaced the screams as I tried to call for help. My door burst open and Lisa came running in.

'I heard you screaming,' she said, shaken. 'Are you OK?'

I shook my head, unable to speak I was crying so hard.

'It hurts,' I finally managed to say. 'I can't breathe.' Lisa went pale.

'I'm going to get help,' she promised and ran off. I sat rocking on my bed, trying to ignore the pain in my lungs, ears and head.

'You're going to be fine,' Star said. I was relieved to hear her. 'Just breathe slowly,' she soothed, and I tried to follow her instructions, even going with the pain. It came in jolts, like shards of glass piercing through me, but I didn't try to block it. That way it didn't seem to hurt so much. I accepted it was going to hurt, and let the pain flow out of my body, rather than trying to rail against it. Lisa came back with Mark, followed by the hotel manager.

'She needs to get to the hospital,' everyone kept saying, but it was 9pm now and dark outside. The only way off the island was by boat, and it was a two-hour journey.

'I don't want to,' I gasped, but Lisa, Mark, the manager and Star all insisted I go. I wasn't going to ignore my spirit guide again, so this time I nodded.

'We need to go now,' the manager said. 'There's a storm coming.'

He began making phone calls and my room filled up with people, carrying a sunbed. There wasn't a stretcher so they were going to use this to carry me to the boat. I would have laughed if I hadn't been in so much pain. Two of the men gently picked me up and laid me on the sunlounger. Then they hoisted me above their heads and began marching across the beach to the jetty, where the boat was moored. I clung to the sides of the sunbed, trying to ignore the pain now ripping through my chest. I was silently crying as they lowered me into the small boat. Mark and Lisa clambered in beside me, along with a woman, who was a nurse on holiday there.

'She's agreed to come with us,' Mark said, taking my hand. 'You're going to be OK, Sis.'

I was shivering by now, even though the night was warm, and my skin was clammy. The nurse took my pulse.

'Hurry,' she urged, but the men were trying to navigate the boat out of the atoll, through the coral reefs. It was tricky, especially at night. Once they'd made it to open water, the captain warned us it was going to be bumpy. I didn't understand. The sea looked like a mill pond, it was so still. But as he went full-throttle, the boat lifted out of the water and sped away. I cried out every time it crashed through a wave as pain shuddered through me. My entire body hurt. It felt like I'd been run over – and I was scared suddenly. I'd known pain nearly all my life, but this was so intense I couldn't believe I hadn't passed out. After a while, I began screaming. I didn't want to but I couldn't stop myself.

'Please slow down,' Lisa begged, but going slower didn't make any difference. Just breathing hurt.

Finally, we moored at Male, and I was taken to a waiting ambulance.

'Give me something for the pain,' I begged, and was relieved to see a giant needle coming towards me. The pain blurred after a couple of minutes, then vanished. My whole body relaxed and I began drifting off. Even going over bumps in the road didn't matter. I didn't hurt anywhere any more.

Mum was there with me. I could feel her energy so close. I opened my eyes and looked straight into hers. She looked exactly as she had when she was alive, her eyes sparkled, and her skin was so smooth. I felt her touching my face, like she had when I was a little girl, and felt her voice whispering and soothing me, letting me know I was going to be OK. I breathed in, and could smell her.

'We're nearly there, love,' she said and I nodded. It was so nice knowing she was there, along with Star, looking after me. Closing my eyes, I clung on to my brother's hand. He and Lisa had jumped in the ambulance with me.

'Mum's here,' I muttered, and everything went black.

A sharp pain woke me, like I was being stabbed.

'Ouch,' I muttered, looking into the face of a nurse, brandishing a needle. I was in a hospital ward, hooked up to a drip. Mark and Lisa were there, their faces white, dark circles etched under their eyes.

'We are giving you antibiotics,' the doctor said. 'You will need an operation.'

I stared at him, bewildered, and then he began to list what was wrong with me. I had a perforated right eardrum, pneumonia and pleurisy. My lungs were infected, which is why it hurt every time I took a breath or exhaled.

More dangerous was the perforated eardrum. Pus was trapped in my inner ear, which could seep up into my brain, or into my blood stream, causing septicaemia, blood poisoning. I needed surgery to clean out the pus, and stop the infection spreading, but they were worried about giving me a general anaesthetic because of the state of my lungs and breathing. I looked at Mark.

'Get me home,' I begged, starting to cry. I didn't want to be operated on here, miles from home, but Mark shook his head. He'd already spoken to the insurance company and they said I wasn't fit to fly home. I had to have the surgery here. But they wanted to wait to give the antibiotics being pumped into me via the drip and injected into my bottom every twenty minutes a chance to work. I was so weak, they were worried.

'We need you to sign these forms,' they said to me and Mark. I couldn't even lift my head up to read, but Mark's face went white when he realized what it meant.

'They don't have the equipment to resuscitate you if anything goes wrong,' he said, and I sighed. He didn't want to sign them, but the doctors were frantic to get the go-ahead. I was deteriorating, and they wanted to make sure the pus didn't reach my brain and cause damage. Poor Mark didn't know what to do. I saw him cuddling Lisa and talking to her outside. He was almost in tears.

'Sign it,' I told him when he came back in. 'I'll be all right.' My voice sounded braver than I felt but I didn't have a choice. I couldn't wait for the infection to spread.

After he'd filled in the paperwork, I closed my eyes, willing Mum and Star to link in with me. I wanted them to reassure me I was doing the right thing. But I was too weak to focus, and I didn't feel them with me. That panicked me a bit, but then it was time to go to theatre, and I clung on to Mark as I was wheeled down.

'Look after me,' I willed as the gasmask was put over my face, and I breathed in the vile-smelling anaesthetic. I had to force myself not to fight. My natural instinct was to snatch off the mask, and get out of there, but what good would that do? I needed the surgery to survive and get better, so I sucked in lungfuls of the gas, and eventually my eyes grew heavy. I was floating. I was so light it felt like I was being carried away, up towards the ceiling. I glanced down and saw myself laying on the operating table, with the surgeons at work. I should have been shocked and cried out, but I was drifting now, and it was relaxing, like bobbing on the sea. I was getting higher and higher, but was fascinated by what was happening to me below.

Suddenly, I saw a bright light, so white it made me blink. As my eyes became used to it, I saw angels and spirit guides surrounding my body on the operating table. The pure white light was coming from the centre of them, and the outer edge was made up of the most amazing colours, all shimmering. Heat was coming from the white light, and it made me feel alive, like I was being charged with electricity.

Then one of the machines made a loud noise. One of the team glanced at it, and I could sense panic in his voice. My heart rate was slow, he said, and my blood pressure was very low. I was deteriorating quickly, but I didn't panic. I watched it all, knowing it was me, but enveloped in calm. The anaesthetist started pumping more drugs into me, along with fluids, but the angels surrounded my entire body now. I was back in my body, and still floating, and I could feel the angels touching me on the operating theatre. I was warm, and happy, and their touches were light, like being stroked with a feather, and I knew I was safe. I was happy to stay there, and didn't want to leave. I wanted to be surrounded and cared for by these angels forever. Then I heard Mum.

'I've missed you so much,' she said, her voice tinkling in my ear. 'Is that really you?'

I could smell her again, and feel her hugging me. Her love radiated through me and I could touch her, too. Her skin was soft, and she looked healthy, and out of pain.

'I don't want to go back,' I told her, looking at my body laid out on that operating table in front of me. 'I want to stay with you.'

It was amazing being in the middle of that heat, and light, and having Mum, Star and the angels there. But Mum was shaking her head.

'You have to go back, Jayne,' she said. 'You can't stay with me.'

I wasn't listening. I didn't have to leave. But Mum was adamant. As the cacophony of alarms and bleeps grew louder, she insisted that I return.

'It's not your turn to pass,' she kept saying, stroking my cheek. 'You need to go back.'

I tried to resist but she was convincing, saying how much my gift was needed, and how I helped the spirits connect with their loved ones.

'You prove that love goes on,' she said, and as she spoke I felt myself drifting down until I was parallel with my body.

'Now,' Mum smiled, and I nodded, grateful I'd seen her again.

'I love you,' I told her and was gone.

Water was dripping on me and someone was crying. It was Mark, and the water was his tears, falling on my face.

'Am I dead?' I croaked, and he hugged me.

'No, you're fine,' Mark said. 'You gave us quite a fright, including the doctors.'

It was foggy, like a dream from years ago, but as he explained what had happened, and how they'd lost me for a few minutes on the operating table, I knew Mum, Star and the angels had saved me. Now I owed it to them to get better, but it was a slog. My system was infected, my chest was so tight, I could hardly breath, and yet I wanted to get out of there. So I ate the soups they gave me, took my medicines and tried to gain enough strength to leave. I was in the hospital for three and a half weeks, but eventually I was given the OK to fly home.

I'd lost so much weight, and was so weak, I had to be taken to the ambulance in a wheelchair. Mark pushed me through security at the airport and looked after me, but airport staff told us I had to prove I was fit to fly.

'I am,' I said, showing them my discharge papers from the hospital and insurance document. They'd paid for me to go in business class all the way home so I could sleep, and I had my medicines with me. Mark had even learnt how to inject me, so he could administer them during the long flight. Finally, it was time to board. Mark carried me to the plane steps.

'She'll have to walk up the steps,' a member of the cabin crew said. Mark was getting frustrated.

'I'm only helping her,' he said, but they insisted I needed to do it on my own.

'We can't take her otherwise,' the stewardess explained. 'It's security in case of an emergency.'

Mark was about to explode, but I touched his arm.

'I'm fit to fly,' I said, and gritting my teeth, I put my hand on the rail and one foot on the first step. It took all my strength and I was shaking with the effort of dragging myself up every step, but I got to the top. I stumbled to my seat, and collapsed.

'Well done,' Mark said, sitting next to me. But I would have done anything then to get on the flight. I was desperate to get home.

The flight was a nightmare. I was dosed up on morphine and all my other medications, but it was still a struggle to breathe. My lungs were on fire, and I rasped with every breath, but I counted down the hours until I was back in London. I'd never been so grateful to touch down in Gatwick, and to clamber into my own bed that night.

It took another month before I felt well enough to do anything, but as soon as I was well enough, I booked to finish my Padi course. I was only one dive away from getting my certificate, and I wasn't going to let all this defeat me. But instead of the Maldives, I did my qualifying dive in a lake in Romford. It wasn't sunny, the water was freezing, and it was dark. I couldn't see a thing, but I was a qualified diver at the end of it, and that was the important thing. I wouldn't let anything, not even nearly dying and having angels by my bed, prevent me from doing what I wanted. I'm stubborn but that's what keeps me going and gives me my drive, and I never want to change that.

That was the first time I'd linked in with angels, and it was very different from connecting to a spirit guide. They are much gentler but have a power that's incredible. I rarely see angels. I don't know why, but when I do, they always have a profound effect on me.

One time I was driving round the M25 with my friend Kerry, coming home from a shopping trip to Lakeside. We were chatting as I approached a junction.

'So I thought we could … woah!' I screamed as a large angel swooped down in front of my mini, almost hitting the bonnet, then flying off. I swerved left, veering off into the exit lane. I tried to get back on the motorway but it was too late. I was already approaching the roundabout.

'What are you doing?' Kerry yelled, panicking. 'You nearly

killed us.'

I fought to get control of the car, and then took a deep breath.

'Sorry,' I panted. 'A bird almost hit us.'

I don't usually lie to friends but how could I tell her I'd seen an angel when she was already protesting that there hadn't even been a bird. She would think I'd gone mad.

'Now we're lost,' Kerry grumbled, looking at me to check I was OK. I laughed.

'Don't worry,' I reassured her. 'We can just go round the roundabout and join the motorway again.'

But when I did, she groaned. There was a tailback for as far as we could see. We sat in traffic for the next four hours. I thought Kerry was going to get annoyed, so turned the radio on. Then we both gasped. There had been a six car pile-up just after the junction where we'd come off and two people had been killed.

I understood exactly what had happened. The angel had saved us. We were just a minute away from that accident and could have been involved. By swooping down and making me serve, we were kept safe.

'Thank you,' I said in my head. That was the second time I'd ever seen an angel, and the second time an angel had saved my life. I haven't seen one since, so I guess that means I'm safe for now.

 *16*

Healing hands

Sheila's sadness wrapped around her like a cloak. Her late father, who was standing just behind her, was desperate to comfort his daughter, but didn't know how to go about it. Her son George was being bullied at school.

'He's fifteen,' I said, seeing him now. He was curled into a ball, crying. 'He's really confused but you have to tell him he's not going mad.' Sheila's eye widened, and she gave a little smile.

'Really?' she asked, and I nodded.

'Your dad's here,' I said. 'He says it's going to be OK.' She didn't look too convinced.

'It's been going on a long time,' Sheila said, her voice tight. 'I don't know what to do.'

I looked at her dad, who was shaking his head.

'It's my fault,' he told me. 'I love George so much I went to see him.'

Sheila gave a sharp intake of breath when I repeated his message. She explained that her son had started hearing voices after her dad died.

'I thought it was because he was so upset about his granddad's death,' Sheila said. She'd tried to find ways to help him, but had become alarmed when he said he could see spirits, including his granddad. 'He was speaking out loud and when I asked who he was talking to, he said to someone in the corner,' she said. 'But there was no one there.'

George couldn't sleep and began having a hard time at school.

'He was a mess, and eventually I took him to the doctor,' Sheila said.

They'd sent him for tests for schizophrenia and diagnosed anti-depressants. Now George refused to go out and had become withdrawn. I asked Sheila for a photo of her son, and as soon as I held it, I saw that he wasn't mad.

'He has an amazing gift,' I told her. 'He's psychic, just like me.' Sheila looked shocked.

'Are you sure?' she asked, and I nodded. 'He could use his ability to help people,' I said. 'He mustn't be ashamed, or think he's crazy. He's clairvoyant.' Sheila's shoulders sagged with relief.

'I'd like to see him,' I said. I didn't normally give children readings, but George was special, and was emotionally vulnerable. I thought if Sheila could bring him to meet me, it might help him. He'd been bullied for so long his self-esteem had gone. He needed help to build himself back up again. I'd always had help accepting my gift. I had Star with me to guide and teach me. Maybe George was suffering so much because he was on his own. I wanted to let him know he wasn't the only one who could see and communicate with spirits.

Two weeks later, Sheila brought George to Selfridges. Emotionally, he was like a five-year-old, so shy and withdrawn he wouldn't even look at me. A handsome young lad, six foot two with blue eyes and brown hair, his energy was soft and pure, but he was surrounded by emotional pain.

'I see spirits, too,' I said. 'It's nothing to be scared of. You just need to be a bit more in control.'

I asked George to come along to a class, and taught him how to open himself up to Spirit, using his chakras, and then how to close himself down, so he could relax and recharge his energy.

'You've lived before,' I said afterwards, careful not to scare him. I could see him in chain mail, and carrying a sword. He was fighting in an open field in medieval times. I could see that he was brave and fought hard, even though he was so young. Then I paused. I saw George being stabbed. The sword went into his chest, piercing his heart, and he fell to the floor. His death was so sudden it didn't hurt, but he was pulled out of his body too quickly. He wasn't prepared for death, and was an unrested spirit.

'I'd like to give you some healing,' I said and handed George an amethyst to hold to open up his mind's eye so I could connect with him on a spiritual level. Then I gently laid my hands on his shoulders and let healing energy flow into him. He was such a gifted boy, but he'd been broken by trauma. The bullying and the self-doubt had destroyed his confidence.

'You will be able to do what I do when you're older,' I said. 'I'm not a doctor but I think you are clairvoyant.'

George began to relax and told me he'd been able to see spirits since he was nine.

'Start believing in yourself,' I told him. I wanted to help him understand how to listen to his inner voice and that seeing ghosts was a privilege.

Afterwards, he looked like a different boy. The stress had gone from his face, and Sheila was smiling.

'Come back for healing as much as you want,' I told them. I didn't charge for it, and was happy to help George. He had a rare ability that needed to be nurtured.

'I hold psychic development classes here every month,' I said. 'Come along.'

I didn't think he'd turn up but I hoped he would. I was sure he could be an amazing psychic if he channelled his energy. So I was really pleased to see him walking towards me the following Saturday.

'Is it OK if I come?' he said, and I grinned.

A dozen people formed the psychic circle, and George fitted straight in. He excelled in the classes, and came a few times. When he stopped coming, I was glad – I'd kept in touch with Sheila and she told me he'd grown in confidence so much he'd got a job.

'It's in a cinema near our house,' she said. 'He loves it, especially as there's one screen that's supposed to be haunted and no one will clean it.'

George offered to do it, and was nervous at first, but over the next few weeks he made friends with the lonely spirit.

'Now he's not scared at all and looks forward to work,' Sheila told me.

He's still only young, but I'm glad George is using his psychic talents. He could be a famous clairvoyant in the future, or he might choose not to use his gift at all. But he's no longer being bullied and is happy, and that's what matters.

I'm very grateful I have healing powers. I like helping people and this is one of the ways of doing that. Not only does it make me feel good about myself, and my ability, but it can literally change people's lives. That's a profound gift to have, literally, in the palm of your hands. So I use it as often as I can, and I never ask for money. I want to give healing help to anyone who needs it, and never turn anyone away.

When a teenaged girl turned up to see me, she seemed distraught. She was tiny, still wearing her school uniform, and just looking into her face made me shiver.

'How old are you?' I asked her gently, and she told me she was 15. 'Have you got someone with you?'

She shook her head. I explained I couldn't give her a reading because she was too young, but she began to cry, and so I sat down beside her.

'Do you want me to give you some healing?' I asked and she nodded. So I took her into my reading room, and laid my hand on her shoulders. Immediately, I realized she'd been sexually abused by a family friend.

'You're in a lot of pain,' I whispered, and she began to sob. The attacks had been going on for years, every time this male friend of the family came to stay. No one suspected a thing and the girl was too scared to tell anyone.

'They might not believe me,' she choked. As she spoke, I became aware of someone else in the room. A young man was standing in front of us, maybe 18, and handsome.

'Your brother's here,' I told the girl. 'He says his name is Tom and that he passed in a car crash.' The girl's shoulders started shaking with fresh sobs, and I let her cry. Her pain and grief needed to come out.

'He's at peace,' I told her eventually. 'But he's saying you need to tell your mum the truth.' The girl's head jerked up.

'No, she'll go mad,' she said. I knew she wouldn't react badly.

'She'll support you,' I reassured her. 'She will be there for you.'

The girl looked at me, unconvinced, but I was sure.

'She will believe you,' I said. 'Tell her what's happened and come back next week.'

The girl promised to come back, and three days later, in she walked.

'You were right,' she said as I gave her more healing. 'She listened, then cuddled me.' I was pleased for her.

'My mum wants to meet you,' she said.

'That would be great,' I said, and looked forward to it. Her mum was a lovely woman who was consumed with guilt.

'I had no idea,' she told me. 'I trusted him. I can't believe he betrayed me like this.' The pair of them came to talk to me and receive healing for a few more weeks. I spoke to them about the possibility of going to the police, and what might happen, but they were adamant they didn't want to prosecute.

'I don't want to go to court,' the girl said. 'I just want to forget all about it.'

It wasn't for me to question their decision. I was just glad the girl had found the strength to confide in her mum and they were helping each other through such a terrible time. Tom came through to see his mum and told her not to blame herself. She couldn't have known the man was going to behave so horribly. It was nice to see the family reunited, and so full of love while dealing with something so dreadful. Even though they decided against seeing justice done through the courts, they had closure. They were a family who wanted to help each other, even in Spirit, and who wanted to prove they were bigger than this man's depraved actions. That took bravery, as well as love, and I was proud to have witnessed it.

Spirits care about loved ones left behind here as much as they did when they were alive. Parents never stop worrying about their children, even if they're grown up and parents themselves. One time, I sensed the spirit of an elderly man around me. He was there for a couple of hours before the phone rang and a depressed-sounding woman asked if she could come and see me straightaway. When she arrived that afternoon, I realized she was the elderly man's daughter. She was terrified, and having marital problems. Her dad told me he was very sad that she was with a man who enjoyed harming her, physically and mentally.

'Please be gentle with her. She's very fragile,' he told me. 'She's lost all meaning to her life.' I knew what he meant – she was suicidal. The spirit told me to reach out and touch her right hand.

'Turn it over,' he instructed, and she jumped as I did so, but it was too late. I'd seen the deep lacerations to her wrist. She'd slashed them, trying to kill herself. I offered her healing but that wasn't enough. This woman needed help, so I talked to her for hours that afternoon, giving her messages from her father, and urging her to seek professional help. 'I can take you anywhere you need,' I said, and she finally asked to be taken to a refuge. I wouldn't normally interfere like that but both her dad and I felt she was in real danger. A couple of days later, the woman came back and asked to join a psychic circle I was running. She became a friend, and would tell me how scared she was of her violent husband and how she'd been so emotionally battered by him she couldn't find the strength to leave. She'd only decided to do something after hearing from her dad through me.

'He gave me the strength I needed,' she said. I passed the message back to her dad, who was incredibly proud he was able to help.

Another time, a girl came to see me who, I could tell, was about to get involved with drugs. There wasn't a spirit or anyone to help her. She was on her own. That's when it's especially hard to persuade someone to change her life.

This girl, Debbie, had been through hell. She'd been used by her father as a sex toy to pass around his friends since she was a young girl. She'd been abused, raped and had undergone three terminations, and she was still only 21. Her mum was an alcoholic, and had been too drunk to notice, or care, what was going on. So Debbie had looked after her little brother, and herself, finding the strength to cope with everything her vile dad and his friends had put her through. Her baby brother had grown up and gone to Australia the moment he was old enough to escape, leaving Debbie to fend for herself. So she'd done the only thing she knew how to do, and made money through flaunting her body.

'I don't sleep with men,' she insisted when I sensed she

worked in the sex industry. 'I only dance.'

I could see she was telling the truth. She was a pole dancer at a club, and did well there. She was popular and made a lot of money, but she wasn't happy. Men wanted to pay just to look at her, and hoped for more, but she always managed to avoid any tricky situations. Now Debbie wanted to know if she'd ever be truly happy.

'You've met someone who's lovely,' I told her. 'You need to be honest with him. He won't judge you.'

She smiled. Debbie was very pretty, with naturally blonde hair and the face of a young girl. She could easily pass for a teenager, rather than a woman.

'Confide in him,' I urged her, 'and you could be really happy together.'

She was shaking her head, and I realized she knew some dodgy men who wanted her to get involved in drugs.

'You mustn't work for them,' I told her. They would only lead her into bad things, like hard drugs or porn. Right now, she had a chance of leaving the sex business and starting afresh. If she went to work for them, she'd be trapped forever.

'Stop taking the cocaine,' I warned her and she blushed. 'It's not helping you.'

Debbie was taking lines of the class A drug five or six nights a week, when she worked. It gave her the confidence to dance around a pole half naked, and to flirt with strangers for tips. She was taking a lot, and if she wasn't careful, she could become hooked.

'You can't change the past,' I told her gently. 'You have to accept it and move on.'

I gave her some Reiki. She needed to revisit the past, have healing and talk through every bit of her life. It was going to hurt, and take a few sessions, but it was the only way she could ever let go of it.

That's when I noticed that Debbie was intuitive, and deeply spiritual. She wore crystal bracelets and a necklace, because she needed to feel protected. I gave her a tiger's eye to hold while we spoke, so she felt safe, and slowly the healing and talking seemed to work. Debbie found the courage to admit what she did for a living to her boyfriend, a builder, and he didn't judge her. He was wary, of course, but he still wanted to see her, and eventually they fell in love. Four months after first coming to see me, Debbie had stopped taking cocaine, which made me incredibly happy, and by six months she'd found the courage to quit her job. She married her boyfriend and they now have a gorgeous baby girl. Debbie dotes on her, and is happy to look after her full-time. She's an amazing mother, who gives her daughter all the love she never had, and then some. I still see her, and she brings the baby in to visit for a cuddle, and I couldn't be more proud.

Debbie had nothing and no one to help her except herself. But she dragged herself off drugs, and learnt some self-esteem.

'I needed to learn to love myself,' she told me lately, 'and that's when I was finally ready to fall in love.'

I hugged her. It could have been a very different story. If she'd carried on the way she was, I'm sure Debbie would have ended a drug addict, working in porn movies, or as a prostitute for men who beat and abused her.

'I had a lucky escape,' she always tells me. 'You're my guardian angel.' But I'm not. She has one of her own, like I have Star. She just hasn't tuned in to her yet.

Not everyone who comes to see me for healing is a victim, though. Couples trying for a baby come along when they suspect a problem, before undergoing IVF. One couple were due to start fertility treatment but first wanted to see if I could help them. I'm not a doctor and have absolutely no medical training, but I can offer healing, and often psychically sense a problem or blockage of energy, which I can attempt to unblock. This couple were in their thirties and had been trying for a family for a couple of years.

'I don't think we can have babies,' the woman said, fighting not to cry.

I gave them a rose quartz crystal each to hold – it's good for fertility – and immediately sensed that he had a low sperm count.

'Doctors say we can't get pregnant naturally,' she said when I told them what I felt.

I gave them both healing but focused more on him. She needed to feel less stressed to give her body the chance to conceive, and I tried to shift the block in his energy. They came back three more times, and the fourth time I saw them, I began laughing as soon as I saw them. The woman was surrounded by pink fertility symbols.

'I'm pregnant,' she squealed and I hugged her. I didn't tell them they were having a girl because I didn't want to ruin their surprise. They sent me pictures, and a lovely thank-you note.

Another woman came to see me after she'd lost her baby boy seven months into her pregnancy. She was, understandably, grief-stricken, and couldn't come to terms with having to give birth to her dead baby. She was so traumatised that she hadn't been able to conceive again, and was now panicking that she'd never have another baby. It had been a year since she'd lost her little boy, and so I talked to her and gave her healing.

She was still very tearful during her second visit, and the third, but by the second month of healing she was pregnant again, and went on to have a beautiful, healthy baby boy. He will never replace the son she lost, but he brought so much happiness into her life.

Sometimes, people don't ask me for help, or even come looking for me because I'm a healer. One time, when my rheumatoid arthritis had become so bad I couldn't keep up with the housework, I advertised for a cleaner, and a woman applied for the job. As soon as she walked towards me I sensed that she was ill. She was in her fifties and guarded when I mentioned her health.

'It won't stop me giving you the job,' I told her. 'I just get the feeling that you're not well.'

Over a cup of coffee, Gail admitted that she had been diagnosed with breast cancer.

'I've had surgery to remove the breast,' she said. 'But it was too late. The cancer's spread.'

Gail now had small tumours all over her body and was terminally ill. So I hired her and on her first visit, after she'd cleaned, I offered to give her healing. Gail and I grew close. I'd listen and laugh at the stories she told me about what she and her two daughters and her granddaughter got up to. She was outgoing, and used to love dancing and partying. Gail knew that the cancer was spreading through her body, but it couldn't destroy her love of life.

I don't know if it was her positive attitude, or the healing, or a mixture of both, but Gail survived another five years. It was still tragic when she died, but she'd had a decade longer than the doctors had predicted to spend with her family, and for her, every single day counted. She managed to pack in more memories than most people do in a lifetime, and enjoyed every moment with her family and friends.

Healing isn't just about mending a broken or diseased body. It can help a broken heart, too. One woman came to see me because, years ago, a boyfriend had cheated on her and she hadn't been able to trust a man since. I gave her healing to boost her self-esteem, so that she could be open to the possibility of falling in love again. She was only in her early thirties and I didn't want her to be alone. I gave her a couple of sessions, and she seemed more optimistic. Then I was booked to do readings at a private party in a pub near my home in Essex, and as I went from table to table, giving five-minute readings, I came across this same woman, sitting opposite me.

'Do you want a mini-reading?' I said, and began to laugh.

'What's so funny?' she asked. I tried to keep a straight face.

'You're going to meet your husband tonight,' I said, and the surprise on her face was wonderful to behold.

'I see a wedding,' I said, and she began shaking her head. But I could see love symbols everywhere, and a ring, showing it was forever.

'He's your soul mate,' I continued, 'but you have to be open to the possibility.'

The woman looked flushed after I finished the reading.

'I need a drink,' she said, heading towards the bar.

I moved on to the next table to give more readings, and it was another two hours before I'd finished working my way around the room. I was getting ready to go and looked around the room for the prospective bride. She was talking to a man at the bar. I waved and she came running over.

'I can't believe it,' she giggled. 'I went to get a drink and started talking to a guy at the bar. We've been flirting ever since.'

I glanced over at the man, then back to the girl.

'He's the one,' I smiled and she blushed.

'Ooh I hope so,' she whispered. 'He's gorgeous.'

A few months later she came into my shop to see me.

'You are the best psychic ever,' she laughed, holding out her left hand. There, on her ring finger, was the biggest, sparkliest diamond solitaire I'd ever seen.

'Congratulations,' I said, hugging her. 'Do I need to buy a hat?' I was invited to their wedding but, unfortunately, couldn't go. But I will never forget them. That was the fastest piece of matchmaking I ever did!

Sometimes clients who come to see me are a bit naughty and try to get me involved with their deceit. One woman, who was lovely, was also married and having an affair. She'd had a baby with her husband, but was now pregnant with her lover's child. She looked so innocent, I could hardly believe it at first, but all she wanted to know throughout her reading was if her lover would leave his wife for her.

'No,' I told her. The answer was unequivocal. He was happy with his wife, and only used Julie for sex. It had been going on for a couple of years, and I couldn't see it stopping.

'I don't see you together,' I told her, hoping it would be enough to shock her into ending the affair. But the following year she came to see me, with a tell-tale bump, and it was the same the year after that.

'You're always pregnant,' I said when she next came, and she smiled.

'I just can't resist him,' she said.

In the end, she had five children, one from her husband and four from her lover, although her poor husband didn't suspect a thing. If I hadn't seen it for myself, I wouldn't have believed it. Julie was tiny, with big eyes and the sweetest face. She looked like butter wouldn't melt in her mouth. But in reality she was living a lie. She wanted to be with her lover, but sadly he didn't feel the same way.

'Fair enough,' I thought. It was none of my business.

I usually saw her once a year, but then Julie booked me to do a reading for her friends and family at her house.

'Is your husband going to be there?' I asked, and she said he would. How could I face him, knowing what I did?

Luckily, there were a dozen guests, so I could take another Psychic Sister, Nina, with me. I spent the entire evening avoiding

Julie's husband. If he came in the kitchen, I went into the dining room. If he went into the garden, I darted inside. It was like something out of a Benny Hill sketch, I worked so hard not to be in the same place as he was. I was exhausted by the end of the night, and grateful when Nina nodded to say she'd given him his reading, so I could relax. I couldn't wait to go home.

Other times, I've unwittingly caused a divorce. A man came to see me in Selfridges, and as soon as he sat down I could tell his wife was being unfaithful.

'She's cheating on you,' I said, matter-of-factly.

'I knew it,' he declared, 'and it's not the first time.'

I tried to see something else to focus on, but everything I saw led to his wife's infidelity.

'How do you know?' the man asked. 'I can't find any evidence.'

He had only his gut instinct to go on, which in this case was spot on. Whenever he raised the subject with his wife, she accused him of being jealous and paranoid.

'She has two phones,' I said. 'She keeps the one she uses to communicate with her lover under the driver's seat in her car.'

In fact, she'd gone to great lengths to keep this phone secret. I could tell that she'd made a special wallet for it, which she stuck right under the seat, so no one could ever find it.

'The sim card is sticky-taped under the passenger seat,' I told him.

If he found them, he would see all the steamy notes they'd sent each other. I hated being the one to pass on the message, but it was coming through so strongly, I couldn't avoid it. He came back the next month to let me know I'd been right.

'The phone was where you said it would be,' he said. 'Once I showed it to her she admitted everything.'

He was now divorcing her, and it was sad that he'd had to find out that way. I thought he would be upset but he was relieved.

'I thought I was being driven crazy by possessiveness,' he said. 'But I was right all along. She was a cheat.'

So, for him, it was a successful reading. He'd found out the truth and been able to move on and leave an unhappy marriage behind. It might not seem as obvious as helping a drug addict, or victim of domestic violence, but I'd managed to give that man some stability and inner peace. He knew he wasn't imagining things and was able to cut himself free from a woman who didn't love him and was a liar. To him, that was the best result possible and he couldn't thank me enough.

 *17*

The colour of people

It would have been funny if the woman sitting in front of me hadn't been trembling with terror.

'She hates me,' she kept saying. 'She's never thought I was good enough for her son. She's put a curse on me.'

I didn't believe in curses. Other people couldn't cast a spell that would make terrible things happen, or bring bad luck, to the victim. But for anyone who believed in the dark arts, a curse was real and powerful. These people were convinced that anything bad that happened to them was the curse playing out in their lives. It didn't matter how many times I tried to explain that they might have lost their job, or missed a flight, or had their flat burgled anyway, and it was nothing to do with any supposed curse, they didn't believe me. And this woman was no different.

'Everything's gone wrong since she cursed me,' she insisted, breaking down. 'Please can you help me?'

I stared at my client, and saw a dark aura around her, so dense it was almost black. That showed the negative energy swirling around her, as well as her fear. In many cultures, a belief in curses, and evil eyes, is inherent. This woman was Muslim, and one hundred and ten per cent sure her mother-in-law had put a curse on her.

'Why would she do that?' I asked, and she explained that her husband's mother had never liked her, and had been irritated to see them so happy together. Soon after marrying, my client had become pregnant and she had given birth to a beautiful boy a month before her sister-in law had had her baby. Her husband's sister and mother were both furious, and insanely jealous, that her child was the first grandson, and had, during an argument, cursed her. From that moment, she believed every little thing that had gone wrong was her mother-in-law's evil doing.

The woman had gone to see gurus in her own country, begging them to lift the curse. A man had said that he would remove it in return for a £3,000 payment, but the woman thought he was a charlatan. Now she wanted me to make sure she was curse-free.

'You have not been cursed,' I tried to tell her. 'But your aura is showing me that you believe that you have so much that you are attracting negative energy and now doubt yourself.'

Her confidence and self-esteem were shattered, and she was terrified about what might happen to her, or her baby.

'The seed's been sown in your mind and your fear is letting it grow, even though it's not real,' I told her. 'If you stop believing, nothing can hurt you.'

I performed a spell, especially to help disperse her fear and cleanse her mind.

'This will make the negative energy go away,' I told her, and gave her healing to boost her confidence. As I focused on relaxing the woman, her aura became lighter, and I knew the spell, and the healing were working.

Doctors examine people's bodies when they go to see them, complaining of feeling unwell. I examine auras. To me, they're as easy to read as a doctor checking for swellings or lumps, or asking a patient to say 'aaaah'. It's the first thing I look at when I start a reading. I work by opening up my crown chakra, at the top of my head, and throwing out what I call a straw to connect with the other person. It's like a beam of light from the top of my head to link up to my client. A white glow begins to emanate from around the person I'm reading, and that's how I know the connection's there – a bit like the light coming on the television when you switch it on. As the connection gets stronger, the white glow changes into a colour – usually pastels – and those colours merge.

The colours are significant – each one has a different meaning – and every psychic has a personal code. Over the years, I've learnt to trust my own interpretation and understanding. I have seen thousands of people for readings, and they often come back to validate messages I've given them, which were usually based on their auras. I also give aura readings where I draw what I see. For me, it works as well as Tarot, clairvoyancy or crystal readings, and is easy to understand.

If someone needs healing, I see green. I often tell clients who are anxious, or need to gain confidence, to visualize the colour green for a few minutes every day, because it will help them to feel more confident, and calmer. Over time, as they heal themselves, their aura will change to a different colour.

If someone has been sexually abused in the past – and a lot of people who've suffered in this way seem to visit me – the colour amber surrounds their heart. Colours aren't always around the head, where people expect them to be. They can be anywhere on the body, but are usually sited around the chakras.

Purple across the top of the head tells me this person is very spiritual, and if the person is very advanced, the colour will be silver. A practising clairvoyant's, or psychic's, aura will be gold.

Pink is the colour of love, but also indicates a marriage or babies. Red shows passion or anger, which are always closely linked. Orange is to do with business and materialism. To me, it's the colour of money. Blue is to do with communication, and there are several different hues. Dark blue shows depression and low self-esteem. Mid blue shows that someone is creative and artistic, and light blue shows me that the person is calm and relaxed.

White shows childlike, pure emotions, while the darker an aura is, the more deep-rooted an issue will be, and it is usually negative, like the woman who believed she'd been cursed.

At the beginning of my psychic journey I always loved using Tarot, but as my confidence grew, and I met new people, I discovered different techniques. The very first time I ever came across aura readings, and drawings, was when I was working in Australia and staying in a B & B with another reader, Suzanne. I was broke at the time, and couldn't afford an expensive hotel, but I'd been booked to give a lecture to a group, and needed somewhere to stay. Suzanne was lecturing as well, and even though I'd never met her before, she agreed to share a room, and share the cost. She was tall, with long black hair and kind eyes.

'Do you want a cup of tea?' she asked, trying to make me feel welcome after a long drive. I shook my head.

'Have you got coffee?' I said and she made me a cup. It was hot, sweet and just what I needed. As we sat sipping our drinks, Suzanne kept looking at me.

'You have the most wonderful aura,' she finally said. 'Can I draw it?'

No one had ever asked me that before, so I agreed, and she took out her pastel chalks and a pad. Fascinated, I waited for her to begin, but her hand froze in midair.

'Star's here,' she said, and the hairs on my forearms prickled. 'I'm going to draw your spirit guide,' Suzanne continued, frantically rubbing her chalks across the paper.

Excitement shot through me as I watched, transfixed, waiting for the face of the woman who'd started me on this psychic journey to appear on the pad before me. But Suzanne guarded the drawing.

'You can't see until it's finished,' she said, instructing me to sit down and not to peek. She was working at the most amazing speed, but it was as if every minute had become elastic, stretching out, forcing me to wait.

'I'm putting the diamond in the middle of her forehead,' Suzanne explained, and I remembered the pentagram that had lit up my old bedroom back in Loughton all those years before. Suzanne's voice sliced through the memory.

'She looks a bit like you,' she said. 'Only her skin has more olive tones.'

Blues, silvers and gold pastels all left their marks on Suzanne's fingers as she drew Star.

'You first met her when you were five,' she said and I nodded.

As she came to life on her artist's pad, Star came through to Suzanne, who started telling me things about my past and myself that no one else knew. She was channelling my spirit guide, bringing her to life on the page and through her own psychic ability.

Finally, she announced I could look at the picture. It was more than a drawing. It was a portrait so sharp and lifelike it looked like a photograph. And there, caught looking straight out at me, was Star, who'd been with me, helping and teaching me to accept and develop my psychic talent, since I was a little girl.

'It's beautiful,' I said, trying not to cry. It was so startlingly accurate, the kindness and wisdom apparent in her brown eyes, that it was overwhelming.

'You're amazing,' I told Suzanne, and she handed me the picture.

'It's yours, to keep you strong,' she said, and I took it gratefully. Of course, I didn't need the picture to remember what Star looked like. She showed herself to me all the time but it was the proof I needed that I wasn't a freak. I hadn't imagined her. Star was with me, and other psychics, people just like me, could see her too. It was comforting knowing that others could connect with her, and see her so clearly they could bring her to life, like this.

'I want to do aura drawings,' I said, and listened as Suzanne told me how to focus.

My first attempts were crude – I'm no Matisse or Monet, that's for sure – but as I drew more and more auras, my portraits improved. The connection was just as strong as with Tarot and crystals, and at the end of each reading I'd give my picture to my client as a keepsake. I'm not as good as Suzanne, who was like a professional artist, but my clients seem to like my drawings.

I still have my picture of Star, and every time I see it, I smile. She looks quite like me, but she never ages. She looked exactly the same when I first saw her as a little girl, and while I've grown up and got wrinkles, she's still as youthful as that first day we met. I'm not jealous. I'm just glad she's here to help me.

As a psychic, I connect to people visually, but I don't just see spirits – I can also hear, taste, feel and touch them. Spirits always appear on the left-hand side of a person, and just before they come through I often shiver or give an involuntary shudder, because I feel cold. Then I see lights twinkling, which become stronger and stronger, and begin to form a face, then a body, until I can see the whole person, just as clearly as if they were alive. I don't always see the spirits – some are shy and don't want to come through – but I always feel them, and see those twinkly lights.

As soon as I've connected, the spirits tell me how they died. I get palpitations in my chest and a pinch in my heart if it was a heart attack, and vibrations in my tummy if it was something gastric that caused their death. I'm particularly susceptible to anyone who passed because of lung cancer, pleurisy or pneumonia, getting a sharp, stabbing pain in my side and a bubbling feeling in my lungs. Spirits who died in an accident or a car crash give me pains in my legs, and I can tell if someone committed suicide because I first get a tightening around my neck. I can even tell how the person did it, through connecting with more and more spirits over the years. Anyone who died of an overdose or drugs makes me feel like I'm choking, and I literally have trouble swallowing. If hanging was the cause, I feel like I have hands squeezing my throat. Of course, there are a million ways to die, but I feel them all, and every day I'm adding to my psychic vocabulary.

I'm lucky to hear spirits' voices so clearly that it often makes me jump. Sometimes I can't believe others don't hear the voices, because they are so loud and clear, but really I'm hearing them inwardly. They give me names and even whole sentences. Some spirits, who lived in different countries, teach me foreign words or phrases, and I don't realize I'm saying them. I can say a few words in Indian and Chinese now, because I've connected so often with people from there, but if it's a complicated message, Star and other spirit guides translate them for me instantaneously. It means I hear the message in English even if it's in Swedish – it's not like I'm at the Eurovision Song Contest!

In every day life, people will always find a way to communicate and be understood, and spirits and psychics are the same. I've understood a sign language since the beginning, and the vocabulary gets bigger every week. If someone is cheating, I see it, literally. If a woman is cheating, I see a pink triangle. If she is the client and her husband is cheating on her, the triangle's blue. If a couple are about to move home, I see a square, and if my client is confused, I see a squiggly line. Gold coins mean money and stability while a grey coin shows someone is in financial distress and about to face hardship.

Crystals act in a similar way – they have their own properties, but there are similarities with other signs and colours. Rose quartz, for example, is always associated with love, as is the colour pink. But pink-and-black speckled rhodochrosite is a very complicated crystal. It helps with hormones and has no tie-in with my colours and meanings.

All these tools are very personal, and something that means one thing for me may mean something completely different to another psychic. We all have our favourites. I love amethyst, but that's because it helps with pain. I wear one around my neck all the time, and it works as well as my medication does for my rheumatoid arthritis. Anyone who knows me can tell how much pain I am in just by looking at my necklace. The more pain, the darker the amethyst; the lighter it is, the more chance there is of me cracking a joke.

My amethyst is purple – no coincidence because that's the colour of spirituality, which is what I deal in all day every day. Spirits don't take the weekend off so neither do I, although no working day is ever the same. One morning I might be dealing, back to back, with clients with emotional issues, or who are just curious to know what's in store for them. Other times I could be healing someone with a phobia, or I could be looking at contracts for some of the world's most important businessmen. I've done everything from pre-nups through to conveyancing and checking business deals. The owner of a

£3.2 billion company came to ask my advice. He was about to buy another firm, and wanted to know if it would all go ahead OK. I told him that it would go ahead, but I saw a problem with the contract.

'There's a paragraph that needs changing,' I said. 'It's been written in a way that's detrimental to your main company, and could cause a problem.'

I could see exactly where the problem paragraph was – the fifth one down on page six. The businessman, who was from China, asked me if I could wait and he rushed over to his hotel nearby to fetch the actual contract. He looked up the paragraph I was referring to and called his lawyer.

'He said you are right,' the man said, smiling. 'You have saved me a lot of money.'

He bowed. I was pleased I could help, and have seen him a lot since then.

Some businessmen seem to consult me more than they do their own staff. I'm quite used to very complicated contracts, as thick as telephone directories, being thrust at me. I'm not a lawyer and don't understand a word of them, but I don't need to. I don't read them. I just know where the problem clause is and tell the client the page number. They take it from there. One businessman, who is quite well known, told me that my advice saved him millions of pounds. If only I was on a bonus …

I'm always happy to help and try new things. One day, a couple of years ago, I had a call from a company who wanted to embrace the psychic world using technology.

'We want to hold the world's first Twitter séance,' a man said.

I liked playing around on my laptop and iPhone, and loved Facebook, but I wasn't on Twitter and wasn't sure how it worked. He explained it was a bit like Facebook, but you could 'follow' celebrities and anyone else you wanted to, all over the globe.

'It's like a massive conversation that you can join in,' he said.

The séance would work by us announcing that we would try to link in with celebrities who had passed. Their fans could give me questions to pass on to the stars in Spirit. It sounded interesting.

'I'm in,' I agreed.

I was to be the only psychic, and the company – Angels Fancy Dress, who provided all sorts of costumes for hire – gave me a list of stars, already suggested by fans on Twitter. The first name was Michael Jackson, which made total sense. He had such a massive following all over the world, and everyone wanted to know what had happened since his death in June 2009 at Neverland. I was a fan of the second person on the list, also a musician – Kurt Cobain, the lead singer with American grunge rock band Nirvana, who killed himself in 1994. The other two names on the list were actor River Phoenix, who had died the year before of a drug overdose outside Hollywood nightclub the Viper Room, and playwright William Shakespeare.

'I ignored him all through school,' I thought wryly. 'Now I have to try to talk to him in front of the world.'

But I was excited really. No other psychic had ever attempted this before, and the appointed date was 31 October, Hallowe'en, so it was getting a lot of attention. In reality, though, it was no different from any other reading. The team from Angels and I sat together, and were joined, via the computer, by strangers all over the globe, who had logged on to us on Twitter. They were going to ask questions while I linked in with the celebrities. I would talk, as normal, and one of the Angels team would type in my answers, so I could concentrate on the connection and not the keyboard.

It's no more difficult connecting with lots of people than it is with one. When I do a live show, literally hundreds of spirits try to give messages to their loved ones. So I took a deep breath, opened up and waited. Anticipation fizzed through the room as the 'tweance' was about to start. I could feel a young man around me. He was handsome, and enormously talented – River Phoenix. A 'tweep' asked if he regretted being an actor rather than a musician. His answer was instant and I watched the man typing it in as I said it – 'I was always a musician. Acting was the job that paid the bills.' River was a kind, honest young man, who happily answered his fans' questions. Then he gave me a message.

'I want my mum to know I am OK where I am. I was abrupt with her at times and I'm sorry.'

It always comes down to this – relationships between parents and children and an overwhelming love that can't be diminished by death. I was proud he'd been open with me and had been happy for me to tell the world. He then spoke about his use of drugs, saying he took them 'to overcome my fears'. But he admitted they can 'destroy and damage' and that he was sorry 'to leave my family in such a devastating way'.

I could feel River had said enough now and had begun to fade away. In his place was Kurt Cobain, and instantly I felt completely different. I had a fuzzy, spaced-out sensation, like cotton wool packed around my face. I was in pain, feeling sick and struggling to breathe. My skin itched, my gums were sore and my eyes dry. I hate feeling like this. Kurt hated it, too, but this is how he felt near the end of his life. It was awful. A fan asked if it was better to burn out than fade away.

'Neither,' Kurt told me. 'If you're clean, you don't fade away, and that's what I wanted to do, to get clean and watch the people you love grow.'

Kurt was fading away now, and so I tried to connect with William Shakespeare. It was such a weak connection, I wasn't sure at first. I realized he was there, and then he was gone. Many people had tried to contact him, but he'd lived so long ago. Instead, I felt someone else step forward, a legend who was ready to talk to his fans.

'Michael Jackson's here,' I said out loud.

It was such a strong connection, it made me reel. He was singing 'Heal The World', and I smiled, hearing his beautiful voice. His energy was young, pure and innocent, not that of a grown man. He told everyone he was happy and at peace now, and insisted his legacy would live on through his voice and his music. His life was complicated, he said.

'I was a man of many masks,' he confessed. 'I don't know if I ever saw the real me myself. But my love was real and my heart sincere.'

Now that he'd passed over he was at peace with himself.

'My masks have all fallen off now,' he went on. 'I am just myself and I feel pure, and I want people to know that. Be happy in your lives.'

He acknowledged that he should have asked for help, and apologized for not being able to tour.

'I'm sorry for letting you all down,' he said. 'I know you will complete the journey for me.'

There were questions still coming for Michael, but I could feel him getting ready to depart.

'He is light and will continue sending love around the world,' I said and then he was gone.

A couple of hours had passed in the blink of an eye, and I was buzzing. You'd think it was exhausting connecting with so many energies, but it was the opposite. It was like I'd been plugged in to the mains and now I was wired. I couldn't sleep for ages, and kept thinking about the evening. I respected all of the artists I'd connected to, and was in awe of most of them. They'd all come through and answered questions from fans, and been so honest. I was proud, and a bit humbled, to have been able to be their messenger.

The tweance hit headlines everywhere, and newspaper, magazine, TV and radio journalists wanted to interview me. I was happy to talk to them, but I hadn't done it for the publicity. We'd pushed technological boundaries, using Twitter, and I'd been able to connect some superstars with their global fans, as well as feel their energy around me. That was enough for me.

Not all readings are that exciting, or important, but they can be extremely funny. A woman came to see me, and I could tell immediately that she had lost her mum. But one message kept coming through over and over again.

'Why is your mum so unsettled?' I asked her. 'Why haven't you scattered her ashes?' The woman looked at me as if I'd gone mad.

'What are you talking about?' she said. 'Of course, I've scattered them – in her favourite place in the woods, where she used to walk the dog.'

I paused, hoping to hear that her mum had understood, but she was indignant, and kept saying, 'Scatter my ashes. Please.'

The woman was almost in tears, insisting she'd done what her mum wanted. She couldn't understand why there was such confusion. I shrugged. I was only the messenger, and could only pass on what I heard. The reading continued, but never really got past that message, which kept cropping up again and again.

'I don't understand,' the woman huffed as she left. Two months later she came back, looking very sheepish.

'I got a phone call a few weeks after my reading with you,' she explained. 'It was the funeral director's, asking me to go and see them.'

When she got there, the funeral director explained there'd been a terrible mistake and they'd accidentally given her the wrong ashes.

'I thought I was scattering my mum,' she said, 'but in fact, it was a stranger.' There was more. 'The worst thing was I had to have another memorial service, but I was too embarrassed to tell everyone there had been a mistake, and we'd cried and said prayers for someone we didn't know.'

So she'd scattered her mum's ashes with just a few close friends and family, and said she felt very close to her afterwards. She knew her mum was the only person who would have made this happen. They used to joke that her mum would be late for her own funeral – well she'd done even better and hadn't been there at all! At that point, I saw the woman's mother by her shoulder.

'She's so happy you finally scattered her where she wanted to be,' I said. 'But who did you scatter the first time?' Her mum and I were both curious.

'We don't know.' The woman shrugged her shoulders. 'It's a terrible mix-up.' No one had come forward, asking where their loved one's ashes were. 'So I guess we'll never know,' she said. I looked around, half expecting the spirit of the John Doe ashes to appear, but no such luck. Some mysteries I can't solve unless Spirit wants me to.

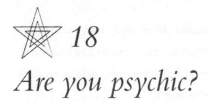 *18*

Are you psychic?

Have you ever looked at the telephone knowing it's going to ring the moment before it does? Do you keep thinking about someone, and see that person's name or relevant signs everywhere – on the side of buses, in the newspaper – and then bump into the person unexpectedly? Can you tell what's wrong with a close friend or family member just by looking? Do you dream about things that then come true?

All of these show you're in touch with your intuition and could be psychic. Of course, it's very rare to be able to communicate with Spirit, but everyone can learn to interpret dreams or psychic tools, such as Tarot cards or crystals.

We're all born with the ability to listen to our gut instinct. It's natural and has helped us survive for so long. I see intuition as our second brain – if we focus on it, we can understand a lot more about ourselves and those around us. We can also tune in to communal or mass feelings, just as when Princess Diana died. How many people felt the overwhelming sorrow surrounding us then? It wasn't just psychics who felt that connection, although many were receiving messages from her as soon as she passed. Ordinary men, women and children were openly weeping on the streets, they were so touched by the loss of someone very spiritual. We felt a collective grief. Imagine if you could tap into that intuition on a daily basis. It's very powerful and works on a subconscious level all the time, bubbling under the surface. You just have to work hard to listen to it.

Most messages come to us in our dreams because we're in an open, more relaxed and receptive state. Often people who are very psychic – whether they know it or not – will see faces or eyes when they close their own eyes before they go to sleep. That's spirits making a connection, ready to come through with messages while you sleep. If you see them, try to develop your ability.

My dreams are incredibly vivid, like watching TV, they seem so real. They're in very bright colour, which is significant to me, so I tune in to it. If dark blue predominates, I know rows and stress are in store. I've learnt to listen to my dreams, so when I get that message, I try to be as relaxed as possible before I leave the house, so that I'm mentally prepared for whatever is waiting for me. Then I'm able to cope better. If I see a lot of green, I'm aware I need healing and could be in extra pain from my rheumatoid arthritis, so I will try to look after myself more.

My dreams are also predictions – I dream about things that are about to happen. These events are more often mundane than dramatic. I may have been thinking about which cooker to buy and in my dream I'll suddenly see it on sale, and when I go to the shop, there it is! When I had to buy new curtains for Psychic Sisters' concession in Selfridges, cream velvet was the fabric I was advised to choose. But whenever I dreamed about them, they were always champagne coloured, and when I went to the shop, they didn't have any cream curtains at all. And what colour did the shopkeeper suggest – yes, you guessed it, champagne, just like my dream predicted. Luckily, they look as good as they did while I was asleep!

I love my dreams, and can stop them, like a video, if I need to get up in the night for a glass of water, and then start them again where I left off as soon as I fall back to sleep. I know most people don't dream as vividly, or as often, as I do, but it's worth trying to write down what you remember of your dream as soon as you wake up, and then interpret what it's trying to tell you.

Developing your psychic ability is like going to the gym to build up your muscles. At first you might be able to do just one sit up, but over time you will be able to do more. It's the same for your intuition. A good way to practise is to do crystal readings.

You need to get a little bag – I have a nice velvet one, but you can use anything – and then buy some small crystals. They're usually about £1 each, and it's a good idea to get eight, each one a different colour. Before you can start reading with your crystals, you have to pre-programme each one with your key word. It's like making up your own code, or crystal language. Different colours and crystals mean different things to different people. To me, a yellow stone represents connecting with Spirit, but it might mean something completely different to you – happiness, because it reminds you of sunny day, for example.

My suggestions for your first crystal bag are amethyst, which is to do with intuition; a clear quartz, which is an open stone for clarity; a blue stone, which represents communication; a rose quartz, which is pink and about love; a green stone for healing; a yellow stone, which represents connecting with the spirit world; an orange one for money and abundance; and a dark brown stone, which is for grounding and stability, and so will show home life. You can have fewer or more crystals, but these eight give you enough variety to do a reading, and as you improve, you can add more and more crystals to your bag.

When you're ready, cleanse your crystals by washing them. I wash mine in tap water but others use spring water. Place them on the windowsill to dry. Then, one at a time, hold each crystal in your hand, close your eyes and focus on it, saying your key word, such as communication for blue, or clarity for clear quartz. When you feel the crystal warm in your hand, pop it into the bag, pick out another one and do the same until they've all been programmed.

You're almost ready to do a reading now, but first you need to open yourself up, to help you connect with Spirit. Close your eyes, take some deep breaths and mentally focus on a bright white light coming towards you. Slowly, feel the light surrounding your entire body, and once you feel calm and safe, call upon your spirit guides or angels to give you help and inspiration. Try to sense their energy as they connect with you.

Now, if you feel ready, relax for ten seconds, then do a reading for yourself, so that you learn how to interpret the crystals. Pick three crystals that you feel drawn to from the bag. These will give you information about yourself. If you have a question, these three crystals will give you the answer through their meaning. For example, if you picked the clear quartz, rose quartz and amethyst, you would have the key words (these are my key words – yours might be different) clarity, love and intuition. So it could be that something is soon to become much clearer about your relationship or love life, and you need to trust your intuition to know how to deal with it, or which way to go.

Keep practising your readings, and after each one close yourself down. You do this by closing your eyes, taking deep breaths and thanking your spirit guides for all their help. As you thank them, imagine a black cloak wrapping around you. Remember to open yourself up and close yourself down before and after readings. The more you do, the easier it will become.

When you start reading for other people, ask them to pick three crystals – more as you become more confident – and tell them to focus on a question as they choose their stones. Your interpretation of the crystals can help form the answer. It's surprising just how accurate your readings will be right from the beginning, for yourself and others. As you add more and more crystals to your bag, the readings will become more complex.

Once you've mastered crystals, you could move on to other tools, such as Tarot or angel cards, and even flower readings. You could also try psychometry, which is where you hold an object and pick up, or read, the emotions of the owner, as well as facts about the piece. It could be a watch, jewellery, a photograph, or even a dog collar or some cloth, anything at all. It works by reading the electromagnetic field, which transfers between the owner and the object every time they have contact.

If I hold an antique necklace, I am able to relay its history, and give details about the person who owned it, and the experiences that person had while in possession of it. If the necklace has been worn, or owned, by more than one person, I can pick up details about all of them, although one may come through more clearly than the others. So you have to remember, the information you're picking up might not be to do with the person sitting in front of you. I once read someone's MP3 player, and kept getting details about Italy, even Italian words. The woman who owned it had fished it out of her handbag, but she'd leant it to her Italian husband for a few weeks beforehand, and I was tuning in to him.

To try psychometry, borrow someone's ring, watch or tie, and hold it. Close your eyes and focus on what you feel and see. Your senses and intuition will come into play the more you relax, so sit very still, breathing deeply, and say what comes into your mind. I bet it will mean something to the owner!

You can even make psychometry into a fascinating game – you can entertain guests after dinner while developing your psychic ability. Gather together some photos, such as holiday snaps, and pictures of people, places, animals and objects from magazines. Put each picture or photo into a plain envelope, according to the number of guests. Seal the envelopes, place them in the centre of a table and ask your guests to select one each. Once they've opened their envelopes, without letting you see what's inside, ask them to visualize the picture and to notice what they feel emotionally and physically, as well as any associations or impressions it may engender. Get them to jot down notes, and you do the same, and then compare. You may be surprised by how similar they are – and all of you will have had a psychic workout!

I love using psychometry because I like to touch something to link in to Spirit and the owner. Everyone has their own favourite way of reading. Some artists draw in crayon, others choose watercolour. Psychics have their preferences, too, and most are better at reading using a certain tool, or are naturally gifted in that area.

A lot of people have natural psychic ability and don't know it, or don't know how to develop it. A woman, who worked on a beauty counter, came along to one of my psychic development classes because she was curious. I was teaching Tarot that morning, and she started doing a reading for another woman in the class. This was the first one she'd ever done but she was amazing, and linked in not only with the Tarot cards, but with the woman's mum in Spirit. The messages and information she passed on were so accurate, the woman was soon in tears – happy to have heard from her mum. No one was as surprised as the make-up girl herself.

'You're fantastic,' I told her, and saw that she was trembling with excitement and nerves.

'I didn't know I could do that,' she said, and I'm sure she didn't. She continued to come to the classes and is so impressive, she now works full-time as a professional reader, and is one of the best Tarot card readers in the country.

I got talking to a sales girl at Selfridges. She had a very fragile energy around her but I could tell from her aura, and from talking to her, that she was a natural counsellor and would make a good reader.

'I think you have a natural psychic ability,' I kept telling her, and she admitted that she was very interested in angels.

She was curious and eventually came along to one of the development workshops. Straightaway she did a reading, using angel cards, and blew us all away. It wasn't long before she gave up her job and became a professional reader.

Not everyone embraces the spirit world as easily as those two women, though. I have a friend who came along to a couple of sessions and was petrified when he realized he was psychic. He'd suspected he might be since he was little, but he had suppressed it. Now, learning how to unlock and develop his ability, he was getting much stronger connections to Spirit, but he didn't like it. One night he rang me, absolutely terrified, because there was a spirit in his bedroom.

'Make it go away,' he begged, and I tried to calm him down.

'The spirit won't hurt you,' I insisted. 'It's just there to give you a message.'

But he was totally freaked out, even though he was a 52-year-old man. Another time, he had linked in with his own granddad in Spirit, but the whole thing terrified him.

'I don't feel in control of it,' he said, and stopped coming to the workshops.

He was scared of the unknown, and that's quite common. My sister Julie was taking a spiritual healing course, and developing her very strong psychic ability. She has always been gifted, but one day, eighteen months into it, she linked a lady with her daughter in Spirit during a reading. She managed to finish the reading, because she realized how important it was for the mother to hear from her lost little one, but Julie was terrified afterwards.

'I don't want to dabble,' she told me.

I tried to persuade her to finish the course, because she'd put so much hard work and time into it, but she wouldn't. She now works in a school, but it's an old one, and so she can feel the energy of spirits there, but she keeps herself closed down.

'I'm too frightened, and never want to see another ghost again,' she told me.

I understand that. I've never been scared of the dead, but for some people it's too much. That's fair enough. There's no point doing something that makes you uncomfortable. But linking in and connecting to Spirit is not at all like you see in horror films. The spirits are mostly there to feel close to their loved ones, and would never harm anyone, or want to frighten them.

I think anyone who's meant to be psychic will be drawn to it eventually, and if it's your destiny, you will end up on that path. I don't think I would have been a psychic if my mum hadn't died. I was happy working in a bar in Tenerife, and had no other plans. But her death brought me home, and after that I needed to be back in Britain and close to my dad and brothers and sisters.

So you can think it's destiny, or you can think that it's the work of my mum, who wanted to be around me. She knew if I developed my psychic ability and began working as one professionally, we would be as close after her death as we were while she was alive. This way, I see her, smell her, talk to her and feel her love, and I help others get back in touch with their loved ones. There's no bigger gift than that – is there?

If you want to learn more about psychic development, why not go along to your local Spiritualist Church. They're free and open to everyone. They helped me enormously on my psychic journey.

If you'd like to come along to one of my psychic development workshops, or have a reading, please get in touch. My website is www.psychicsisters.co.uk

Author's acknowledgements

I want to thank the following people: Octopus Publishing Group and especially Liz Dean, for believing in me when others wouldn't – many others made promises but never quite delivered when push came to shove.

Karen Pasquali Jones for giving me my first column in a weekly magazine (I loved all the free press trips!) and for all your help with this, my first, but not last, book.

Paul Kelly (always in the right place at the right time) and Selfridges for such an amazing opportunity.

My family for their continued love and support.

Star, my spirit guide – without you I wouldn't be the psychic I am. I guess we will meet in your world one day.

Thanks to all my reception staff who keep my business running when I am either away on holiday or at home sleeping (I love my bed so much!), and to my amazing team of readers, you are all great and I love you all.

My biggest thanks I save for my fiancé Leigh Ryan, for your continued love and for always wanting to protect me from the world. You are more intuitive than anyone I know, and if you would just let me teach you, you would make a brilliant clairvoyant. Last but not least, I would like to thank every one of my clients, old and new – I have laughed with you, and I have cried with you. I hope I was able to help you all during those hard times.

And to my readers – without you, this book (the first of many, I pray) would be a waste of hard work.

God bless each and every one of those mentioned, and if I have missed anyone out there is always the next book.